Religion and Philosophy

ROYAL INSTITUTE OF PHILOSOPHY SUPPLEMENT: 31

EDITED BY

Martin Warner

CAMBRIDGE UNIVERSITY PRESS

CAMBRIDGE
NEW YORK   PORT CHESTER   MELBOURNE   SYDNEY

Published by the Press Syndicate of the University of Cambridge
The Pitt Building, Trumpington Street, Cambridge, CB2 1RP
40 West 20th Street, New York, NY 10011-4211, USA
10 Stamford Road, Oakleigh, Victoria 3166, Australia

*A catalogue record for this book is available
from the British Library*

ISBN 0 521 42951 X (paperback)

Library of Congress Cataloguing in Publication Data

Religion and philosophy/edited by Martin Warner
p. cm.—(Royal Institute of Philosophy supplements: 31)
Includes bibliographical references and index.
ISBN 0521 42951 X (pbk.)
1. Philosophy and religion. 2. Religion and ethics.
I. Warner, Martin. II. Series
BL51.R347 1992   91-43788
200′.1—dc20   CIP

Origination by Michael Heath Ltd, Reigate, Surrey
Printed in Great Britain by the University Press, Cambridge

Contents

Notes on Contributors

Renford Bambrough is a Fellow of St John's College, Cambridge, Sidgwick Lecturer in Philosophy at the University of Cambridge, and editor of *Philosophy* (the journal of the Royal Institute of Philosophy). He was President of the Aristotelian Society for the year 1989–90, and is the author of *Reason, Truth and God* (Methuen, 1969) and *Moral Scepticism and Moral Knowledge* (Routledge, 1979).

Cyril Barrett, SJ is Reader in Philosophy at the University of Warwick. He edited Wittgenstein's *Lectures and Conversations on Aesthetics, Psychology and Religious Belief* (Blackwell, 1966) and is the author of *Wittgenstein on Ethics and Religious Belief* (Blackwell, 1991).

Michael Durrant is Reader in Philosophy of the University of Wales and from 1988–91 was Chair of the Board of Studies for Philosophy at the University of Wales, College of Cardiff. He has written on topics in the Philosophy of Religion, Philosophical Logic and Ancient Philosophy, and is the author of *Theology and Intelligibility* (Routledge, 1973) and *The Logical Status of 'God'* (Macmillan, 1973).

Peter Geach, FBA is Emeritus Professor of Logic at the University of Leeds and was Stanton Lecturer in the Philosophy of Religion at the University of Cambridge from 1971–74. Books of his relevant to the symposium to which he contributes in this volume include *Three Philosophers: Aristotle, Aquinas, Frege* (with G. E. M. Anscombe; Blackwell 1961), *Reference and Generality* (Cornell, 1962), *God and the Soul* (Routledge, 1969), and *Truth, Love and Immortality: An Introduction to McTaggart's Philosophy* (Hutchinson: 1979).

A. Phillips Griffiths is Professor of Philosophy at the University of Warwick and the Director of the Royal Institute of Philosophy. His 'Kant's Psychological Hedonism' in *Philosophy,* April 1991 is relevant to his paper in this volume.

Peter Lamarque is Lecturer in Philosophy at the University of Stirling. He has written extensively on aesthetics, literary theory and the philosophy of language, edited *Philosophy and Fiction: Essays in Literary Aesthetics* (Aberdeen 1983), and is the Philosophy editor of a forthcoming *Encyclopedia of Language and Linguistics* (Pergamon).

Herbert McCabe, OP teaches theology and philosophy at both Blackfriars, Oxford and the University of Bristol. He is a former editor of *New Blackfriars* (the journal of the English Dominicans); his most recent book is *God Matters* (Chapman, 1987).

Notes on Contributors

Stewart Sutherland is Vice-Chancellor of the University of London, Professor of the Philosophy and History of Religion at the University of London, and Chairman of the Council of the Royal Institute of Philosophy. He is a former editor of *Religious Studies* and the author of *Atheism and the Rejection of God: Contemporary Philosophy and The Brothers Karamazov* (Blackwell, 1977), *Faith and Ambiguity* (SCM, 1984) and *God, Jesus and Belief: The Legacy of Theism* (Blackwell, 1984).

Roger Trigg is Professor of Philosophy at the University of Warwick. He has written widely on basic themes in Philosophy and his recent books include *Understanding Social Science* (Blackwell, 1985), *Ideas of Human Nature* (Blackwell, 1988) and *Reality at Risk: A Defence of Realism in Philosophy and the Sciences* (2nd edn Harvester, Simon & Schuster, 1989).

Martin Warner is Senior Lecturer in Philosophy at the University of Warwick and was the founding Programme Director of the University's Centre for Research in Philosophy and Literature. Recent publications include *Philosophical Finesse: Studies in the Art of Rational Persuasion* (Clarendon Press, 1989) and (as editor) *The Bible as Rhetoric: Studies in Biblical Persuasion and Credibility* (Routledge, 1990).

The contributions by the above were first presented to the 1991 Royal Institute of Philosophy conference for VIth Form and Further Education teachers at the University of Warwick. Most have been extended or otherwise modified in the light of discussions at, or initiated at, that conference.

Introduction

MARTIN WARNER

I

Religion, Reason and Reality

'Religion' is standardly defined either as 'a particular system of faith and worship' or as 'recognition on the part of man of some higher unseen power as having control of his destiny, and as being entitled to obedience, reverence, and worship' (OED 1971: II 2481). The focus, that is, may be on religion either as a practice or as a framework of ideas and beliefs, but the two elements are interdependent; faith and worship are unintelligible without some idea of that to which they are directed, and religion's characteristic conceptions are such that certain practices and responses are seen as appropriate—even mandatory. Indeed, it has often been argued that 'religion' derives from *religare* ('to bind'), witnessing through its very etymology to the characteristic religious sense of binding obligation, a duty of 'obedience, reverence and worship', as well as of social bonding. The contemporary notion of religion as a matter of free human choice is of comparatively recent development, strongly influenced by secular pressures; more characteristic of classic religious consciousness is the implicit demand mediated through both Old and New Testaments: 'I have chosen you, says the Lord of hosts', 'You have not chosen me, but I have chosen you' (Haggai ii 23; John xv 16).

The form of religion that has most significantly shaped Western culture is that of Christian theism. The reference in the dictionary definition to 'some higher unseen power' is a partial reflection of the characteristic religious denial that all our experience can be wholly understood in terms derived from the physical, temporally structured, universe, and the corresponding affirmation that there is that which transcends the literal application of such categories—to be spoken of only, if at all, by means of images, symbols, narratives, parables, metaphors, models and analogies; to use traditional language, a religion takes the dimension of mystery seriously. A theism is that type of religion which claims that all its images, models, analogies and so on of this transcendent mystery are ultimately reconcilable *both* with each other (God is one) *and* with every feature of human (and non-human) existence (God is Creator). It is for this reason that theisms which, like

1

Christianity, include among its dominant images those like that of a loving father find the 'problem of evil' so intractable. A virtually universal characteristic of theism is the practice of worship, directed to this transcendence understood as a unity—referred to in English by the word 'God'. Christian theism is distinguished from other forms by its dominant images and narratives, which are focused in the biblical records.

From Classical times, of course, it has recurrently been objected that any such 'higher unseen power' lacks reality, and one and a half centuries ago Ludwig Feuerbach more specifically argued that the idea of God is a projection of human beings' own ideals for themselves—that far from man being made in God's image, God is made in man's (Feuerbach 1957). The standard *riposte* is that human experience points beyond itself, and that inability to recognize this represents a form of imaginative, intellectual and perhaps moral blindness; God has 'left not himself without witness', though many fall into the category of 'the blind people that have eyes' (Acts xiv 17, Isaiah xliii 8).

The religious scepticism of the Enlightenment which Feuerbach inherited was part of a wider sceptical movement of thought whose problems are notorious. It may be possible to limit evidentially significant experience to a clearly delimited set of 'hard data' commensurate with the categories of contemporary physical science, but this not only removes God (and any objective morality) from view but also other people; the sceptical puzzle of how we can properly ascribe mental functioning and inwardness to others simply on the basis of our own experience has unnervingly close structural similarities with religious scepticism (see Plantinga, *God and Other Minds* 1967). Further, the Enlightenment attempt to displace God while retaining meaning and value in human life now seems distinctly problematic; developments over the last quarter-century have only served to reinforce the interest of the proposal by David Jenkins (now Bishop of Durham) that we should reverse the Feuerbachian analysis: 'The reduction of theology to anthropology was a prelude for reducing anthropology to absurdity. If we have grounds for re-understanding anthropology as theology, we may yet have hope that we can be rescued from the Absurd' (Jenkins 1967: 79). How an individual responds to these claims and counter-claims tends, not unreasonably, to be significantly affected by how far one finds oneself impelled to take seriously intellectual demands and/or aspects of one's own experience that cannot be seriously responded to or expressed in non-religious terms without what seems to be distortion.

To 'find oneself impelled' is a very different matter from making a criterionless choice; coming to terms with one's own experience in this way is more like 'the kind of unmethodical, accumulative procedure by which a mass of sensitive responses are precipitated into a philosophical belief, . . . a notion embodied in Pascal's *esprit de finesse* or Newman's illative sense' (Quinton 1985: 20–1; for a detailed exploration and analysis of such *finesse* see Warner 1989a). Anthony Quinton's juxtaposition of philosophical belief and Cardinal Newman suggests that what we have here may fall under the categories both of 'reason' and of 'faith', and so indeed it proves. Renford Bambrough's opening paper in this volume is concerned to show that there is no sharp opposition between reason and faith for faith is itself a mode of reason. There are of course traditions which seek to separate them sharply, and the term 'fideism' was coined in the nineteenth century for a form (later, any form) of irrationalism that sets (and upholds) religious faith *against* reason. But such positions are very difficult to render coherent, gaining what measure of currency they have through neglect of the analogies between religious and other forms of belief and by positing an implausibly constricted notion of rationality.

Here, as elsewhere, tidy-looking dichotomies can lead to severe oversimplifications of the complexities of our knowledge, beliefs and understanding. To break their hold on us it is helpful to compare a wide range of particular cases, and this Bambrough sets out to do. To take just one of his examples, faith in one's doctor can be well-grounded and reasonable or the reverse; it would be very odd to retain that faith when shown it was unreasonable by setting faith against reason—the contrast between reason and faith that is plausible here is in fact between two forms of rationality, between one's reasonable confidence in the doctor's judgment and the reasons available to oneself, apart from that judgment, for following the course of action the doctor recommends. As Bambrough points out, this is a 'typical case of trust or confidence being allowed to outweigh what you come to regard as superficial and dangerous grounds', but such a contrast presupposes the falsity in this instance of any analogue of fideism, and helps to broaden our conception of what counts as 'rational' and of how reason may constrain us. Assembly of example after example supports the case for 'counting faith and hope and trust and confidence as rational faculties'.

Further, as Roger Trigg insists in his response to Bambrough's paper, my continuing faith in my doctor as a source of future guidance is not well placed if he or she has died suddenly this morning; not only must the object of my faith be reliable and worthy of trust, but 'whatever I have faith in must exist for my faith to be justified. . . . Faith can persist as long as it is believed that its object is real, but it logically cannot survive an acceptance of its unreality'. In generalizing the case in this way Trigg is criticizing the application to the concept of belief of the influential doctrine of anti-realism which, at least in the forms here considered, has considerable internal difficulties.

Introduction

In general terms, realism is the doctrine that that which we encounter exists quite independently of us—although not necessarily in the form that we conceive of it—and that reality (whether physical, temporal, mathematical, mental, moral, religious or whatever) is therefore independent of our conceptions of it. In the words of its most sophisticated critic, Michael Dummett: 'Realism is a definite doctrine. Its denial, by contrast may take any one of numerous possible forms, each of which is a variety of anti-realism concerning the given subject matter: the colourless term "anti-realism" is apt as a signal that it denotes not a specific philosophical doctrine but the rejection of a doctrine' (Dummett 1991: 4). Dummett is concerned to undercut the framework of the traditional debates by recasting them in terms of meaning theory; he makes no claim to have resolved any of them, merely to have provided a 'prolegomenon', but warns that 'there is little likelihood of a uniform solution to all of them' (15). He certainly has no tendency to see the difficulties he has identified in the logical and meaning-theoretical presuppositions of classical realism as undermining traditional belief in God (Dummett 1991: 348–351; see also Dummett 1978: xxxix).

In less cautious hands, however, matters are very different. For Richard Rorty, for example, anti-realism should replace realism globally through a fairly straightforward inversion; we should reject the notion that human experience points beyond itself, drop 'the very idea that the world or self has an intrinsic nature' independent of our concepts and languages and, with it, 'the idea of languages as representations'—mediating an independent reality to us; such notions represent 'a remnant of the idea that the world is a divine creation' whose nature is given by that which is transcendent of us, and should be abandoned (Rorty 1989: 21). With these notions, as Trigg points out, go the traditional ones of truth and rationality as well—which places the status of Rorty's claims and apparent arguments, as he is well aware, in a somewhat paradoxical light. One is reminded of Dummett's toying with the Berkeleyan argument 'that anti-realism is ultimately incoherent but that realism is tenable only on a theistic basis', a thesis he reluctantly set aside on the ground that he (and by implication we) do not 'know nearly enough about the question of realism' (Dummett 1978: xxxix). For Rorty the paradoxes, or apparent paradoxes, are a function of the ways our languages and assumptions have been distorted by our picture of 'the mind as a great mirror, containing various representations—some accurate, some not' which it is the business of reason and method to correct and improve; for 'it is pictures rather than propositions, metaphors rather than statements, which determine most of our philosophical convictions' (Rorty 1980: 12).

This last claim can be illustrated in his own case by the way he is apparently held captive by another picture, that of rational argument requiring 'common commensurating ground' (1980: 364). In theory he is critical of the notion that there is 'no middle ground between matters of taste and matters capable of being settled by a previously statable algorithm' (1980: 336–8), but in urging his case he trades on just such a tidy-looking dichotomy: 'There is no way, as far as I can see, in which to *argue* the issue. . . . There is no "normal" philosophical discourse which provides common commensurating ground. . . . If there is no such common ground, all we can do is to show how the other side looks from our own point of view', and on this basis the only criteria of acceptability are 'agreement' and 'convenience' (1980: 364–5; 1982: xl–xliv). Recognition that 'algorithmic' reason is inadequate to the task of correcting and improving our representations of the world plays a significant role in his rejection of the picture of the 'great mirror', whose development he attributes to the Enlightenment but whose roots are far older; once again, an inadequate conception of reason has had irrationalist consequences. (For fuller discussion see Warner 1989a, esp. 28–30 & 359–364; also 1989b.)

Despite the problems of his position, and his explicitly atheistic stance, Don Cupitt invokes Rorty in support of his own brand of religiously tinged global anti-realism, which is the main target of Roger Trigg's paper. Cupitt proposes a radical revision of the traditional conception of God, and with it of religious belief: for Rorty, as we have seen, we need to abandon 'the very idea that the world or self has an intrinsic nature', they are language-dependent; analogously, Cupitt claims that 'language creates reality', and therefore 'like us, God is made only of words. . . . We can no longer distinguish clearly between the sense in which God creates, the sense in which language does, and the sense in which we do' (Cupitt 1990: ix–x). There is a clear break here with the traditional religious belief that we are created and sustained by God rather than the reverse, and that consequently God's choice is prior to that of his creatures and human creativity dependent on the Creator. This form of anti-realism also subverts the presuppositions both of Feuerbach's analysis and of the Bishop of Durham's counter-proposal; neither the reduction of theology to anthropology nor the re-understanding of anthropology as theology have the consequences anticipated if world and self, God and we, are on the same ontological level; indeed, given the paradoxes inherent in the positions of both Rorty and Cupitt, the prospect held out by David Jenkins of 'rescue from the Absurd' would appear to be a mirage.

Roger Trigg is concerned to show that these paradoxes undermine the possibility of both reason and faith, and point to an underlying incoherence. Beliefs, like emotions and other elements of our mental lives, have targets; they are directed towards items which we may misunderstand or which, indeed, may not exist—but when there is such misapprehension recognition of the error standardly modifies the belief or emotion; where it does not do so we have irrationality and neurosis. Except in the special case where a belief is self-directed, there is a clear distinction between the person believing and the item believed, between subject and object. As Bambrough points out in his criticism of William James' 'Will to Believe', while in certain cases the psychological fact that someone believes something will happen may causally influence the course of events in such a way as to render that belief true, this goes no way towards showing that 'faith in a fact' can help create a fact in any more radical sense; my belief in my doctor cannot in any other sense justify that confidence. Trigg argues that global anti-realism of the Rorty/Cupitt brand is irreconcilable with the distinction between subject and object, and hence the recognition that reality is independent of our conceptions of it, that appears to form an essential presupposition of our mental lives when we are not consciously fantasizing. In proposing that we credit their claim that the presuppositions of belief be rejected Rorty and Cupitt undermine their own rhetoric (for on their own terms it can hardly purport to be rational argument): 'There is a distinction between the person with faith and the object of faith. My faith in God must involve trust in someone beyond myself.' And more generally, far from it being the case that language creates reality, 'Language is the tool of our thinking and not its prison'.

II

Logic and Language

A number of responses are no doubt possible to this challenge. One would be to begin to draw distinctions between the ways in which reality is and in which it is not independent of our conceptions of it. Another would be to drop blanket arguments for what I have characterized as 'global anti-realism', and in sober Dummettian style accept that 'there is little likelihood of a uniform solution'—realist or anti-realist—to the full range of metaphysical problems with respect to which these categories have been invoked. But in neither case is there any guarantee that some variant of the radical claims of which Rorty and Cupitt seek to persuade us will emerge from the analysis, either as a general conclusion or more specifically in the case of religion. In the present context a more promising line of approach is opened up by considering the notion of constraining limits which the picture of language as a prison evokes.

Part of the appeal, both of religious fideism and of Cupitt's reinterpretation of the concept of God in terms of the creative powers of
language, derives from the traditional insistence that the mystery at the
heart of religion transcends all our categories. This mystery is characteristically spoken of not as one item amongst others but as that in
which all things, ourselves included, subsist—'in him we live, and
move, and have our being' (Acts xvii 28)—and on which all depends;
the religious attitude, therefore, tends to go together with a sense of
radical contingency, of the need to take seriously the question 'why is
there anything rather than nothing?', the rejection of any answer in
terms of that about which a similar question could be pressed, and
hence a conception of God as that which does not fit into any of our
explanatory chains which explain how things are—as radically transcendent, the 'that than which no greater can be conceived' of St
Anselm's *Proslogion*.

Those who believe that their experience has given them some
immediate (if radically limited) knowledge of God are commonly
termed 'mystics', and the types of claim and language made by those
whose credit has stood the test of time testifies to the radically
anomalous character of that about which they write. Similarly, the term
'mystical' ('*das Mystische*'), is used in Wittgenstein's *Tractatus* to point
in the same direction: 'It is not *how* things are in the world that is
mystical, but *that* it exists.' (1961: para. 6.44), and here too the
linguistic problem is insisted on: 'There are, indeed, things that cannot
be put into words. They *make themselves manifest*. [*Dies zeigt sich*.]
They are what is mystical.' (para. 6.522). We are told in the Preface that
language has a limit, 'and what lies on the other side of the limit will
simply be nonsense' (1961: 3); nevertheless, notoriously, the penulti-
mate paragraph of the *Tractatus* declares that its own propositions 'are
nonsensical' and yet can be used—when 'transcended'—to 'see the
world aright' (para. 6.54); it would appear that in its own terms the
work exemplifies *das Mystische*.

Whether or not the image of language as a prison is generally helpful,
the recurrent sense that it has limits which constrain us but which the
religious impulse seeks to transcend is frequently present in the phenomenon of mysticism. Here we find particularly strong resistance to
any attempt to reduce the religious mystery to ordinary human categories, like having faith in one's doctor, and yet the wish to use these
categories—for they are the only ones we have—to speak of it. This
tension is addressed in the discussion between Herbert McCabe and
Cyril Barrett on the logic of mysticism. As Barrett points out, it is a
mistake to think of mystics as 'a special breed of religious believers' for,
at least on the Wittgensteinian analysis, 'anyone who has a religious
experience is a mystic' and similarly, while any philosophy of religion

'must be firmly based on a logic of religious language' it should also recognize 'that religious language is itself mystical, that is, an attempt to express the inexpressible'. This helps to explain why religious discourse generally is notoriously elusive, with the consequent appeal of fideism, irrationalism or simple agnosticism and its apparent openness to the charge of unintelligibility; nevertheless, the issues are particularly sharply focussed in the writings of those whom Barrett terms 'professional mystics'.

The very concept of 'mystical experience', in the narrower sense of the contemplation written of by the Church's 'mystical doctors', appears to bear on the issues both of realism and of the elusiveness of religious language. St John of the Cross, for example, writes of the 'secrecy' and 'indescribability' of mystical contemplation in such a way as to suggest its transcendence of at least the main part of our conceptual apparatus: 'For, as that inward wisdom is so simple, so general and so spiritual that it has not entered into the understanding enwrapped or cloaked in any form or image subject to sense, it follows that sense or imagination (as it has not entered through them nor has taken their form or colour) cannot account for it or imagine it, so as to say anything concerning it'; in some cases the soul may be 'clearly aware that it is experiencing and partaking of that rare and delectable wisdom', but not in all; further, apparent expressions of that experience are for St John no guarantee of its reality. (1978: 'Dark Night of the Soul', 429–30). The discerning spiritual director needs to rely on a complex and overlapping range of indicators: some will relate to the possible contemplative's spiritual history and current disposition, such as general aridity and inability to meditate not brought about by obvious causes; others to apparent effects of the experience, such as detachment, self-denial, humility and, more generally, great tranquillity and virtue; a third set are perhaps best understood as general standing conditions, well summarized by Benjamin Gibbs (1976: 538) 'It is absurd to ascribe mystical contemplation to someone who has not willingly embraced a life of suffering for Christ's sake'.

To say that someone fulfils all these criteria is not to say that he or she is a true contemplative, but there does nevertheless appear to be a conceptual connection between the ascription of the contemplative state and recognition of the fulfilment of these conditions, such that it is necessarily true that the meeting of these criteria affords evidence that an individual is 'experiencing and partaking of that rare and delectable wisdom'. There is a clear analogy here with the notion of a 'criterion' employed by Wittgenstein's *Philosophical Investigations* in its discussion of our ascription of certain mental states and processes, when 'An "inner process" stands in need of outward criteria' (1953: I para. 580; see Kenny 1967: II 258–61); given the close structural similarity noted above between scepticism about other minds and scepticism about God, it is perhaps hardly surprising to find St John's pattern of thought matching so closely one which Wittgenstein was later to identify as that which was required to meet the sceptical challenge (1953: I paras 354–5).

There remain, however, problems about the God-ward reference integral to St John's analysis, concerning such claims as that in the case of contemplation 'the Holy Spirit infuses it and orders it in the soul . . . without either its knowledge or its understanding' (1978: 'Dark Night of the Soul', 428). The ascription of contemplation could be shown to be false—in technical language it is 'defeasible'—for the evidence affords only a presumption, and even if the presumption is not rebutted it may nevertheless be false, for in the last analysis it is God alone who 'knows the secrets of the heart' (Psalm xliv 21). For St John, in infusing the gift of contemplation God is 'imprinting' his footprints upon the soul, and '"Thy footsteps shall not be known"' (431–2; quoting Psalm lxxvii 19). The reality of a person's state, it would appear, may in this instance be different from what either that person or anyone else believes to be the case on the best evidence available, a claim which is easier to fit into a realist than an anti-realist frame of reference, but in either case it raises problems of intelligibility: as Wittgenstein puts it in his discussion of mental functioning and the law of excluded middle: '"God sees—but we don't know." But what does that mean?' (1953: I para. 352) Here we encounter once again the elusive character of religious language.

Barrett's claim that religious language generally 'is itself mystical' follows from the general account of mysticism provided by Herbert McCabe in the paper to which he is responding. McCabe focuses on the account of theology provided in the work of St Thomas Aquinas, one of the classic benchmarks of orthodoxy for the Catholic Church, arguing for a convergence between St Thomas' conception of the divine and that of the mystical to be found in Wittgenstein's *Tractatus*.

For St Thomas the key notion for exploring talk about God is that which he refers to as '*esse*', 'to exist' (the infinitive of the verb 'to be'). We grasp the notion of existence not as we do ordinary concepts, discovering through experience which items do and which do not fall under the concept, but through learning to say what is the case; 'we do not have a concept of existence as we have a concept of greenness or prevarication or polar bears'. Standardly, whatever exists does so as some kind of thing—as a polar bear for example—and falls under a specific range of concepts, which preclude it from falling under another set; if a polar bear then neither naturally green nor a dodo. Enquiry about the existence of an item or class of items (for example, dodos) operates by asking whether there is anything which falls under a certain

Introduction

concept and hence not under others; 'given the natural world we understand the natures of things by contrast with what they are not'.[1] However when we are considering the existence of the world itself, not when we are considering why it should exist in this way or that but its existence as such, this analysis is impossible. If we press the question 'why is there anything rather than nothing?' it is at once apparent that no answer could be satisfactory couched in terms which enable the same question to be asked of that which the answer posits, in terms which pick out one more item as instantiating a given concept—for why should that item itself exist? Whatever is posited, it clearly cannot be understood as having existence in the ordinary way; in McCabe's formulation: 'the Uncreated exists without *having* existence.'

It is the existence of the world as opposed to the possibility that there might not have been any world at all, the 'gratuitousness of things, that St Thomas calls their *esse*. . . . In thinking of the *esse* of things we are trying to think of them not just in relation to their natural causes but in their relation to a creator'; the grammatical difficulty of the expression (the 'to be-ness' of things) echoes the difficulty of the thought. Wittgenstein it will be remembered, wrote 'It is not *how* things are in the world that is mystical, but *that* it exists.' (1961: para. 6.44), and McCabe suggests that 'he is engaged with the same question as St Thomas is when he speaks of *esse*. As St Thomas distinguishes between the creative act of God (which we do not understand) and natural causality (which we do), between creation and trans-formation, Wittgenstein distinguishes the mystical from "what can be said".' But at this point, of course, the two diverge. For St Thomas, it is 'the *esse* of things that leads us to speak of God—which, for Wittgenstein in the *Tractatus*, cannot be done', for the relations between concept and object, and between predication and quantification, adumbrated above govern 'what can be said', and beyond that we are left with that which makes itself manifest in our use of language but cannot be described in it—a domain which, as Peter Geach points out in his paper, extends to all language, not just religious discourse. For Wittgenstein, we approach the mystical simply by recognizing the limits of what can be said.

But, McCabe points out, St Thomas does not give up so easily. If both he and Wittgenstein are addressing the same question, then the mystical is not a particular specialized area of theological interest but

[1] The legitimacy of McCabe's appeal to the notion that things have 'natures' is supported by both Durrant and Geach, who are agreed that we cannot 'take it for granted that this medieval stuff has long since been shown worthless by the labours of John Locke'. Geach's fullest defence of this aspect of the Thomist account may be found in Anscombe and Geach 1961: 'Aquinas', sect. 2.

central to the whole biblical tradition which he seeks to understand. St Thomas 'wholeheartedly agrees that we cannot say what God is [in the sense of specifying the Divine nature], and he sets himself the task of understanding how we could speak of what, being the source of *esse* itself, is outside the scope of the world of existents'. This he sees as possible for two reasons: we can understand what God is not (and this may form the basis for positive statements as well as negative), and we can use words to point beyond what we understand them to mean. The second point is illuminated by the common phenomenon of the analogous use of words, when we use a word in different contexts with systematically different senses without simply making puns; much theological language works in this way: both a dog and his master may be faithful, but in different senses appropriate to the nature of each; if God is faithful it must be in a manner appropriate to the divine nature, but since we cannot say what God is (in the sense of specifying his nature) in affirming God's faithfulness we must also admit that we do not know what faithfulness would be in God, we cannot specify the precise sense of the term in this context. Not all religious language works like this, much of scripture uses metaphorical imagery which may be as properly denied as affirmed (God is both a strong rock and not a rock); nevertheless, such non-literal language needs to be underpinned by the analogical if it is to retain referential status, to be more than just 'the art form of a particular culture' (celebrating, perhaps, a 'God made only of words'), but rather to represent 'part of our access to a mystery beyond our understanding which we do not create'. On McCabe's account, in this underpinning we are 'taking language from the familiar context in which we do understand it and using it to point beyond what we understand into the mystery that surrounds and sustains the world we do partially understand'.

Cyril Barrett, accepting the main lines of this account, applies it more specifically to the language of those normally termed 'mystics'. Both Meister Eckhart and Nicholas of Cusa offend against the normal logical and linguistic rules in 'trying to express the inexpressible' while maintaining 'epistemic discretion', and Barrett points to the close analogies between the 'learned ignorance' of Nicholas and Wittgenstein's account of the inexpressibility of absolute values in his lecture on ethics. Barrett notes, but does not address, the possibility that this insistence on God as transcendent may be in some tension with those aspects of the biblical tradition that speak of miracles and other forms of divine intervention, and seeks to reinterpret the Scholastic account of theological analogy in terms of modern theory. Instead of the traditional claim that in analogous predication 'words are used with partly the same meaning and partly a different one', with its radically problematic presupposition that the meanings of words can be divided into

11

parts, Barrett proposes that when we use a word analogically the *meaning* remains the same but the *sense* is different because the *use* to which it is put varies; we may apply the word 'good' in different senses to all sorts of items—food, equipment, works of art, people, God—but the constant meaning which traverses all its uses is that it is an expression of approval. Not knowing God's nature we do not know the sense of the word 'good' in applying it to him: 'we do not know in what the goodness of God consists. All we know is that he is something to be approved of and is, in some way, the source of every kind of goodness'. In using such terms analogically of God we are 'pushing out beyond the boundaries of language into the unknown. But we are doing so by means of language and of what is known. And we are doing so in order to understand the known better.' Further, 'to press from the known into the unknown via the problematical . . . is a natural tendency in all human beings that are intellectually aware'.

This account is certainly suggestive, representing a significant advance on the older tradition, but nevertheless incorporates more than one problematical element. The notion of 'use', for example, appears to require further analysis if it is to enable us so to differentiate meaning from sense as to account for analogical variation in the senses of words. There is indeed one powerful contemporary tradition, in the formation of which the *Tractatus* played a significant role, which explains meaning in terms of truth conditions—understood as being specifiable without essential reference to the users of words—and thereby makes a sharp distinction between meaning and use (see, for example, Davidson 1967 and 1978); but it has its own internal difficulties and further problems when applied to theology. In any case it is not the approach preferred by Barrett, for whom meaning can be explained by reference to such items as 'expression of approval', which is very difficult to analyse without reference to what users of language do; linguistic expression of approval appears itself to fall into the category of linguistic use, and if this is right the proposed distinction between meaning and sense can only be secured by means of a more fine-grained distinction, or set of distinctions, between different types of use.

Further, to the extent that calling God 'good' signifies approval related to his being 'the source of every kind of goodness', there may be an echo of the difficult doctrine of necessary likeness between a (primary, *per se*) cause and its effect (encapsulated in the Scholastic tag: *'omne agens agit simile sibi'*). But even without this encumbrance—which is not strictly necessary to Barrett's thesis—there is the problem that if God is the source of 'the world of existents' this appears to go beyond the claim that he is 'the source of every kind of goodness': 'I form the light, and create darkness: I make peace, and create evil: I the Lord do all these things' (Isaiah xlv 7). If 'good' is glossed in terms of that to which we give our approval, then the claim that God is 'something to be approved of' is less securely related to the assertion that he is 'the source of the world of existents' than to the apparently narrower one that he is 'the source of every kind of goodness'; yet on the Thomist account given by McCabe and endorsed by Barrett the former assertion is primary. Nevertheless, Barrett's insistence that we know that God is something to be approved of is far from gratuitous for, as we have seen, it is fundamental to religion that its central focus should be 'entitled to obedience, reverence, and worship'—and it is difficult to see how one could could coherently deny that that which was entitled to one's obedience, reverence and worship was also entitled to one's approval.

The incipient tension this seems to suggest between the requirements of philosophy and of religion in what we may say of God is brought into focus in the debate between Michael Durrant and Peter Geach. Both agree that 'holding God to be transcendent does not mean having to regard the grammar of the word "God" as isolated or unique or inscrutable', and Durrant's first move is to bring out the incoherence of the suggestion that the word should be treated as a logically proper name, having reference only but no sense, no describable mode of presentation of that which is referred to: 'I may only claim that I am pointing towards something in my use of an expression if I can at least offer *some* description of what it is I am pointing towards'. Further, if the claim that God's nature is inexpressible is interpreted to imply that the word 'God' has no sense then we cannot even refer to God in such a way as to be able to 'claim of *Him* that *He* did certain marvellous acts'. In fact, Durrant and Geach agree, 'God' is grammatically a common noun with a sense (Durrant explicating the notion of 'sense' as a dimension of meaning given in terms of use). But when Durrant attempts to specify the meaning of the word in terms of its use in practice, he encounters the concern noted by Barrett lest those uses which involve God's transcendence be incompatible with those which follow biblical tradition in maintaining God's action in the world; is the word 'God' as used by philosopher-theologians such as St Anselm— with his famous formula for God as 'that than which no greater can be conceived'—compatible with the faith associated with Abraham, Isaac and Jacob, the biblical Patriarchs?

Durrant considers the thought experiment proposed by Thomas Morris that we should somehow discover 'a less than Anselmian being, an individual who was very powerful but not strictly omnipotent, very knowledgeable but not literally omniscient and very dependable but not altogether immutable, etc., had created our universe and was responsible for the existence of intelligent life on earth', and that this individual 'had been the one to call Abraham out of Ur, to speak to Moses, and to send the prophets' etc. Should Jews and Christians

rightly refuse to call him 'God'? If not, this would appear to show that
the concept of God explored by the philosophers is not the Judaeo-
Christian one. Morris argues that such a being could not be God on the
ground that the object of worship in the Judaeo-Christian tradition is
understood as the ultimate reality responsible for the existence and
activity of everything else, and the being specified could not be this.
Durrant objects that the case is, in effect, rigged; that both philosophical and biblical traditions certainly understand God as maximally great
or perfect, but that there are very different types of great-making
properties. God is conceived in the philosophical tradition represented
by St Anselm as immutable, impassible, atemporal and metaphysically
simple, but it could be argued that the conception of God as 'a
ceaselessly changing, perfectly responsive temporal agent continually
interacting with created, temporal beings' is closer to the biblical
conception, and that this *could* be the ultimate reality. If the word
'God' is to be shown to have a coherent meaning, the apparent incompatibility between the properties standardly attributed to the God of
Anselm and those witnessed to in the Bible—that God is personal,
merciful, loving, forgiving, etc.—needs to be overcome. We might
argue, for example, that while human persons are certainly not atemporal the concept of the personal in its application to God is that of
conscious purposive agency—and it is far less clear that this could not
be atemporal. Through such analysis, thinks Durrant, it may be possible to show that the supposed divide between the God of the Philosophers and the God of the Scriptures is a mirage—it has not yet been
shown that the traditions are incompatible—but such an endeavour can
only be properly conducted on a detailed, case-by-case basis.

Peter Geach is sceptical about the presuppositions of any such
endeavour, since the terms in which the divide has been set up are to
him suspect. The proposed thought experiment fails because we cannot
give a coherent account of how we could ever make the discoveries
proposed. Again, like McCabe and Barrett he draws attention to the
orthodox insistence that we cannot know God's nature, pointing out
that for St Thomas we can only say what God is not; to characterize
God as immutable, impassible and atemporal is in each case to say
something negative, to say God is metaphysically simple is to deny of
him 'that sort of inner distinction or complexity which is to be found in
creatures', and 'greatness', understood as 'perfection', is not itself a
perfection. Further, St Anselm developed his account out of the biblical tradition, himself writing one of the classic discussions of why God
became man, and the scriptures themselves witness to the claims of not
only Christian but also pagan philosophers; true knowledge of God,
even on Christian terms, is not confined to scriptural revelation. Philosophy as well as Scripture can help show that in some cases λατρεία (the

fullness of worship which may be paid to God alone as distinct from δουλεία, the reverence permissible to created beings) is misdirected to that which is incompatible with the meaning of the word 'God'; further, to the extent that the proposed idea of a 'ceaselessly changing, perfectly responsive temporal agent continually interacting with created, temporal beings' is incompatible with what philosophy shows could coherently be said of the source of 'the world of existents', any worshipper of such a being is worshipping a false god, a god made in man's image.

Durrant accepts much of this, attempting in further notes to suggest how the debate needs to be modified to take account of Geach's intervention; the discussion exemplifies, indeed, how live philosophical dialectic can clarify difficult issues. It also indicates, however, that such issues interconnect in complex ways, for if we may relate biblical and philosophical traditions to each other in the manner proposed we need to be able to give an account of how we are to understand biblical as well as philosophical talk about God. Both McCabe and Barrett draw a firm distinction between theological discourse, literal though analogical, and the religious language of much of the Bible which is metaphorical or otherwise figurative; but if the identification of the God of the Philosophers with the God of the Scriptures is achieved by reading scriptural figures in terms of the theological analogies which are taken to underpin them, the circularity involved may be felt to trivialize the matter unacceptably.

My own contribution on the proper interpretation of scriptural and liturgical language provides a prolegomenon to the full addressing of this issue. The overall strategy is to attempt to undermine the standard and dangerously tidy-looking dichotomy between theological and religious discourse, while leaving room for the necessary distinctions that provide its motivation, through analysing metaphor itself as a mode of analogical discourse, and through exploring the rules of use employed in the more religiously demanding areas of biblical discourse which enable us to discriminate between acceptable and unacceptable inferences.

Traditionally the Bible was read as scripture as well as literature; this involved interpreting it as to some extent a 'lawless' text, with the inbreaking of the divine Word characteristically being marked by the contravention of human literary and linguistic rules, hence the use of 'dark sayings' in the Gospels and the notion that scripture has multiple senses; St Augustine wrote of its 'salutary obscurity'. Enlightenment theories of language as governed by rules whereby each proposition properly relates the ideas designated in a determinate manner challenged this approach as unintelligible—lawless texts were meaningless—thereby strengthening the tendency to read the Bible

15

'suspiciously' rather than 'faithfully'. However I argue that a judicious integration of certain contemporary analyses of language—which relate meaning to use, metaphor to analogy, and inference to context—provides logical space for the phenomena pointed to by the notion of 'lawlessness'. Since the widespread and normative use of scripture in Christian worship presupposes a 'faithful' attitude to the passages employed, these analyses also have a bearing on current controversies concerning attempts to renew the language of worship.

In his reply Peter Lamarque, while broadly sympathetic, raises certain objections to my account which he seeks to modify and extend by pointing to some of the analogies between reading the Bible 'as literature' and 'as scripture'. In criticism, he is concerned lest the emphasis on metaphor take insufficient account of scripture's cognitive function—its capacity to convey propositions assessable as true or false—and lest the emphasis on context presuppose access to matters which are unavailable to the reader save through strategies of unacceptable circularity; more generally, whether philosophy of language reaches its limits in considering sacred texts, and the attempt to analyse them in terms of the paradigms of secular language is in principle unable to illuminate the putative inbreaking of the divine Word.

In place of my paradigm of the creative metaphor he proposes that of the literary work, not to collapse scripture into literature, but to provide a parallel: 'just as . . . the aesthetic dimension of a literary work cannot be reduced to any particular feature of the meaning of its component sentences . . . so the scriptural dimension of a sacred text is not itself reducible to naturalized features of its meaning'; literature 'demands a distinctive mode of response' defined by 'the conventions of interpretation and evaluation constitutive of the practice associated with the [literary] institution'; similarly with the reading of a text as 'authoritative Scripture'. This is not to reduce scriptural language to the art-form of a particular culture or tradition or institution; on the contrary, 'theological realism, i.e. a commitment to the reality of God and the referential status of religious language (and metaphors), is quite compatible with taking an institutional view of the spiritual dimension of sacred texts'.

I find much of Lamarque's extension valuable; there is indeed a complex interrelationship between the religious institution which designates texts as scriptural, those texts themselves, and the readers who accept this designation—and this interrelation helps determine what it is to read those texts 'as scripture'. Indeed, the reciprocity of this relation needs to be taken very seriously; the believing community, in varying degrees, both determines the texts and is determined by them; it not only judges how to read the texts, but also sees itself as under judgment by them—for the scriptures have a crucial role in the regulation and definition of the very faith that informs the canons for reading them. At this level, the potential circularity Lamarque is uneasy about in my account is embedded in the very rules of the institution to which he appeals.

This helps account for a fact whose implications are, I think, far-reaching for the 'institutional' account—that the institution itself is subject to change. Indeed, the still unresolved debate about norms of scriptural interpretation lay at the heart of that institutional division we call the Protestant Reformation; any account of these matters needs to take account not only of the Enlightenment, but also of the Reformation (and Counter-Reformation). Further, the contemporary problems besetting attempts to bring the requirements of worship into conformity with those of biblical criticism reflect fragmentation within the believing community itself. If one simply appeals to institutional norms, one must press the question 'Which institution?', and without something like the set of considerations I advance one may have difficulty in avoiding some form of relativist fideism.

Lamarque is certainly right to insist that any account of scripture which, like mine, gives prominence to the notion of metaphor must take proper account of scripture's cognitive function, but this does not appear to be impossible; live metaphors are not themselves statements, nor can they be reduced to them, but even if—in traditional realist fashion—truths are taken to be statements that correspond to the facts, it does not follow that metaphors cannot communicate such truths. Scripture's cognitive function, indeed, points to a disanalogy between scripture and literature that appears to lend my account some support. Hermeneutics, the theory and practice of interpretation, developed originally in relation to religious and legal texts because here it was particularly important that meaning be correctly interpreted; one's salvation, or at least life and liberty, could be at stake. Many of its established procedures were transferred to literature when this became, for other reasons, the subject of critical scrutiny; this may well have brought about some distortion, hence Lamarque's concern that 'those who come to literature with theories of meaning . . . get led into one form or another of reductionism'; but to use this perception to allow the colour to flow back, as it were, and reduce the importance of the concept of meaning in biblical hermeneutics to the level appropriate in literature would appear to be reading the Bible 'as literature' in a rather strong fashion. To read 'as scripture' we need to take account of the fine-grained 'atomistic' level of meaning relations as well as Lamarque's preferred institutional one.

At either level, of course, one is dealing with human structures, linguistic or institutional, where the divine dimension can only be discerned by the eye of faith. Hence the (Augustinian) insistence of my paper that the spiritual state of the reader is relevant to recognizing 'the Word incarnated in the word'; the believer tests the text of scripture against his or her own experience, but in the full knowledge that that testing may be as much a judgment on the believer as on the text. The thought that one could escape circularity here would appear to be a version of what orthodoxy regards as the heresy of Pelagianism; in Christian terms, grace is always needed to break the circle—this, one might say, is one of the institutional norms. No doubt the interpretive paradigms I propose are not specific to religious language but, to quote perhaps the most profound twentieth century student of these matters, 'though religious faith deals with mysteries which are *sui generis*, because God himself is absolutely unique, at the same time we expect religious mysteries to bear some analogy with natural realities, because they are revealed in the stuff of our human experience.' (Austin Farrer 1976: 'Inspiration: Poetical and Divine', 45).

·

III

The Moral Dimension

Whether morality is to be regarded as simply a 'natural reality', or whether it and religion represent varying forms of the mediation of the transcendental to human experience, is of course controversial. Wittgenstein, it will be remembered, linked the two as being essentially inexpressible—at least with respect to their 'absolute' character. There is a tendency, no doubt with notable exceptions, for those disinclined to take the religious dimension seriously to naturalize moral phenomena, and for the religious to seek to harmonize the two sets of demands. Much philosophical ink has been expended over the former endeavour, but in the present context it is of less interest than the latter.

Religion, as we saw at the start, is a practice with a sense of binding obligation at its heart, a duty of 'obedience, reverence and worship'. Now it is the business of morality to regulate practice, and its obligations also present themselves as binding and as absolute. Given that religion and morality do not appear to be identical, the question arises of the possibility of conflict between them. It is certainly true that individuals and groups have often believed it their religious duty to act in ways that those outside the circle of faith have found morally abhorrent. Similarly, individuals and groups have found themselves morally impelled to act in ways that to the religious are blasphemous. But it remains possible that in such cases some or all the parties are in error. The powers of human self-deception, not least in moral matters, are apparently inexhaustible; the proper authentication and interpretation

of religious experiences and sacred texts are notoriously delicate matters, some aspects of which have already been touched on; and it is even
possible, as Geach insists, to worship a false god.

If both religious and moral demands are absolute, some such diagnosis is essential if absurdity is to be avoided. But can it be avoided?
The proper test here is to consider what an individual can coherently
believe, and this is the subject of the concluding discussion—'Religion
and Ethics'. There would indeed be radical conflict if we believed
ourselves to have a clear picture of what God wills and found this in
opposition to our moral beliefs. But the central question pressed by
both Stewart Sutherland and Phillips Griffiths is: How could we
possibly come to have such a clear view of the will of God, apparently
arrived at without reference to our moral sensibilities?

Sutherland considers a range of relevant examples, starting with the
classic one of Abraham's projected sacrifice of Isaac—which
Kierkegaard (or, more precisely, his *persona* Johannes de Silentio) saw
as exemplifying the clash between the realms of the religious and the
ethical. He suggests that the fact that we often do find ourselves in
dilemmas where a decision is required in advance of certainty is 'one
mark of what it means to talk of the limits of finitude', but that such
dilemmas may be purely moral. To construe those cases which depend
on 'a clash between religious and moral premises' in the way
Kierkegaard proposes, however, is misconceived, for the alleged
'religious' premise is always related to a picture of God which itself
needs to be justified—and one dimension of this justification needs to
be moral. The meaning of the word 'God' is such that it is analytically
true that if something is the will of God it is morally good—one
remembers St Anselm's 'that than which no greater can be conceived'
and the dictionary's claim that religion's central focus is conceived of as
being 'entitled to obedience, reverence, and worship'. To claim this
analytical connection, however, is not to claim that God *as conceived
by any particular theology or individual* always wills the good; rather, it
is 'to assert a fundamental belief about the ultimate compatibility and
indeed inter-dependence of moral and religious beliefs'. Dilemmas like
that of Abraham should not be seen as disputes about the relative
priority of the religious and ethical realms, but rather of the options
facing the individual 'in the light of the claim that the decision made
should reflect the will of a God who (analytically) wills the good'.

The difficulty of establishing, in any given instance, the truth of the
claim that God wills something immoral has affinities with Geach's
claim, with respect to Morris' thought experiment about a limited god,
that we cannot give a coherent account of how we could ever make the
discoveries proposed. Phillips Griffiths takes the matter one stage
further, pointing to the problems not so much of finding a counter-

example to the analytical connection between God and goodness proposed by Sutherland, as of discerning what would count as discovering a counter-example. The New Testament claim that 'by faith Abraham, when he was tested, offered up Isaac' (Hebrews xi 17; see also James ii 21–3) may (perhaps) be read as providing the Christian believer with warrant to regard Abrahamic faith as exemplary, but Kierkegaard's treatment of the Abraham story is so riddled with anachronism as to render the example useless for his purposes; the fact that the God Christians worship is the God of Abraham, Isaac and Jacob does nothing to show that the god of Kierkegaard's fantasy is not a false one. Further, the appearance of a radical conflict between faith and morality in Kierkegaard's account depends on his defective Kantian view of the nature of ethics, whereby to act morally is to act from the conception of abstract rational law as such, as opposed to acting from an interest in anything; since the religious believer acts from an interest in God, this opens up an opposition between religion and morality which Kierkegaard exploits. Kant's account of ethics, however, is not only philosophically problematic but runs counter to a careful reading of the Gospels. Peter Geach writes of ways in which philosophy may mount a legitimate critique of false religion; Phillips Griffiths provides an example where scripture may be used to mount a powerful critique of false philosophy.

Again, the claim that it is analytically true that if something is the will of God it is morally good needs non-linguistic justification if it is to be more than trivial; in Kantian language, the analysis requires an intellectually significant prior synthesis. Sutherland proposes that the claim asserts 'a fundamental belief about the ultimate compatibility and indeed inter-dependence of moral and religious beliefs' which appears to amount, as Phillips Griffiths argues, to the belief that 'if we reflected long and hard and well enough . . . our religious and moral beliefs would then be compatible and interdependent'. But such a belief implies 'that such reflection leads us nearer to the truth; and that the truth is, that what is really the case regarding God's will is compatible with what really is morally good'. And this, of course, is incompatible with global anti-realism.

But not only may religion have a bearing on ethical and metaphysical theory, it may also play a legitimate role in moral judgment. The moral attitude may be inherent in, and hence help constitute, the religious one, but the latter may also illuminate the former; there is the possibility of two-way traffic in the process of reflection adumbrated by Phillips Griffiths. As Sutherland points out: 'what someone might regard as a moral absolute might be modified as a result of growth of religious insight or by a process of reflection on religious teaching.' Here, once again, the tidy Kantian dichotomy—dependent on a particular conception of moral autonomy that so often lies behind debates in this area—is misleading. Kant holds that 'Even the Holy One of the Gospels must first be compared with our ideal of moral perfection before we can recognize Him as such' (1925: 30). To this it may be objected with Basil Mitchell (1980: 152–3):

> It is absurd to suppose that the fisherman of Galilee—when he made the confession: 'Thou art Christ, the Son of the Living God'—had compared Jesus with his ideal of moral perfection (just as it was before any encounter took place) and had satisfied himself that he had, so to speak, achieved the required standard. He had, of course, judged for himself, and in judging he exercised moral insight, but he could not himself have preached the Sermon on the Mount.

Mitchell proposes for an analogy 'the process by which, as Eliot maintains, a great artist creates the standards by which he is to be judged', and indeed T. S. Eliot's own *The Waste Land* provides a case in point; its impact derived in large part from the way it was perceived as at once standing in a positive relation to established ideals and yet enlarging and transforming them in a manner relevant to the readers' experience. Both in religion and in art, the criteria here are elusive but not beyond reasoned consideration, given a suitably rich conception of reason, and allow for their own self-transcendence in ways that have their own forms of objectivity. But the analogy should not be pressed too far. For the realist strain that runs through religion, brought out in its moral dimension by the claim that what is really the case regarding God's will is compatible with what really is morally good, points beyond the artistic level. As Herbert McCabe points out in the concluding words of his paper, despite their elusive status such literal yet analogical assertions as that God exists, that God is good, and that God is the creative cause and sustainer of our world witness to the religious conviction

> that the riches of religious imagery are more than the art-form of a particular culture (though, of course, they are that) but are part of our access to a mystery beyond our understanding which we do not create, but which rather creates us and our understanding and our whole world.

21

Reason and Faith—I

RENFORD BAMBROUGH

What is the difference between reason and faith? The question is framed in what I would call 'the treacherous singular'. The structure of the question implies a particular form of answer and makes other assumptions about notions that occur in the same region of our network of thoughts and understandings. If I were happy to play this game I might reply in kind by offering a simple formula purporting to sum up my own answers to the cluster of questions that are implicit in the simple form given above. The form makes the question and the answer appear more straightforward than they are. Perhaps I might answer in the questioner's style by stating the conclusions of my paper in these words:

> A simple idea is at the heart of my paper, but one that is hard to absorb and to live by in one's wider thoughts about reason and faith. The simple idea is that faith is itself a mode of reason. This means that there cannot be a sharp distinction between reason and faith, whether or not one tries to express such a distinction in the treacherous singular, or perhaps in the impoverished plural, a mode of expression in which a few separate but simple factors are identified as *what faith is* or *what reason is*.

If we pursue the initial question in the more complicated style that the varieties and pluralities now promise, we seem to be in danger of saying that there is no distinction at all between faith and reason, except that faith is only a *species* of the *genus* reason.

The treacherous singular is busy at its destructive work throughout our explorations, as philosophers, of the terms and concepts in which we think about thought, examine our beliefs about beliefs, enquire into the nature of enquiry. The scope and intricacy of what I called the network is indicated even by a fuller list of characteristic philosophical over-simplifications drawn up in the same form as our initial distinction between reason and faith. What then are the differences between each of the following pairs of familiar notions?

Reason and Experience
Reason and Feeling
Reason and Emotion
Reason and Revelation
Reason and Authority

Renford Bambrough

Reason and Instinct
Reason and Imagination
Reason and Choice
Reason and Intuition
Reason and Insight

So far Reason is a party to each of the alliances or conflicts that these pairs of terms may call to mind. No doubt there are many other distinctions to be drawn between Reason and other individual concepts. There are also, as a few examples will show, similar pairings in which the place occupied in the first examples by Reason is filled by another term that is akin to it as well as capable of being distinguished from it.

Proof and Persuasion
Logic and Rhetoric
The Head and the Heart
Natural Theology and Revealed Theology
Prose and Poetry
Science and Art

A new complication now arises: what about the relations between Reason and the concepts occurring as its various surrogates in these lists of distinctions? When Reason is contrasted with Imagination rather than with Emotion, is the 'Reason' then being examined the same as or different from what it is in the other case and in other cases? The same type of question arises over the relations between the various terms which occupy the 'Reason' position in some of the distinctions: Logic and Science and Proof all differ from Reason and from each other, and in the same manner there is a need for comparison and contrast between terms in the right hand of each column: Persuasion and Rhetoric and Instinct and Imagination.

Each of the distinctions in my list, taken by itself, is at risk of being an oversimplification of a complicated scene. Surprisingly, and invaluably, when we bring a range of such simplifications together they serve to remind us of the great elaboration of the structure of our speaking and thinking about the human understanding, and of the things that it is concerned to represent.

But our own generalizations too are in danger of leading us into the kind and scale of oversimplification against which we have been protesting. So let us take our own advice and say how some concentration on fairly minute particularities may give us a more highly focused view of our eponymous distinction—between Faith and Reason—and of how a piecing together of many similar threads may be seen to compose a tapestry of thought and understanding.

24

Faith in a doctor or driver, or in the foundations of a building, is not ordinarily groundless. Faith is (at least in these contexts) a mode of rational response. If it were not, then we should be tangled in the paradoxes and confusions of William James's 'will to believe', which will be dealt with later.

Religious faith is not so far from satisfying the same conditions as the waving of the flag 'Faith and Reason' may lead us to expect. If we seek to understand a person's faith and its relation to reason and knowledge, whether polemically or eirenically, we are likely to hear reference made to the *authority* of a book or a tradition or a church or a Pope or a prophet. And if we ask what is the ground of that authority, we are not usually told that it is groundless. That would be to fall into a fool's mate before the enquiry was well begun. A defender of the or a faith usually knows better than to lower the drawbridge for the convenience of the enemy.

Do you have faith in your doctor? If you say no, this may be because you *lack* faith in him. But it may be because you question whether the word 'faith' is as suitable as, say, 'confidence' or 'trust' for the particular frame of mind that you evince when you believe your doctor to be careful, responsible, well-informed, conscientious. Whether you call it trust or faith or confidence, the settled belief that your doctor will do all that he can do for your benefit satisfies the terms of my initial simple thought: it is—in ordinary cases—a well-grounded and reasonable faith or trust or confidence. This fact about it is brought into relief when we think of precisely the context in which it is most plausible to *contrast* it with a rational response. Your reasons for your confidence may include facts like these: you know that he is a qualified and experienced practitioner, not too old or too weary of well-doing to apply his knowledge to your need; he has always taken seriously your own uninformed description of what ails you; you have rarely or never in a long association found him hasty or casual or impatient with you or with other members of your family or your friends. Against such a background, if the doctor startles and discomforts you by a sudden ruling on the state of your heart or arteries, and instructs you to change your manner of life, or to undergo risky surgery, you will be likely—even if you do not immediately agree—to take his advice because you trust him not to give you bad advice on such a matter.

This is surely a typical case of trust or confidence being allowed to outweigh what you come to regard as superficial and dangerous grounds for disregarding the advice of a professional person. You cannot see for yourself that you must act in this way or that, but you have rational confidence in your adviser. This inability to *see* is highly characteristic of faith in any context; but the example also shows that we are not concerned in such cases with a contrast between reason and groundless faith, but with an assessment of the weight of the reasons for accepting certain advice and the weight of the reasons for disregarding it.

The same pattern recurs in numerous everyday examples: you trust the Forth Road Bridge or a Boeing 707 without understanding but not without reason. A child clings trustingly to her mother's apron strings; the mother relies on an older child to find his own way to and from the corner shop in safety. Mountaineers have confidence in the ropes from which and on which they depend. A driver does not set out to cross the Sahara without believing in the engine under the bonnet.

These examples could be multiplied indefinitely without departing far from a recurrent pattern, and an assembly of them is sufficient to make out my case for counting faith and hope and trust and confidence as rational faculties, not accurately to be contrasted sharply in the manner of the reason/faith or reason/feeling dichotomies. They are not trivial examples. All the same, they are not sufficiently important and wide enough in scope to satisfy some philosophers, and especially some beginners in philosophy, that they are serious and substantial enough to offer a path towards truth and understanding of the role to be filled in the realms of religion and morals by the seven or eight great dichotomies. It is only because of our piecemeal, case by case exploration that we can produce counter-examples to the requirements that philosophers typically wish to impose by their definitions and theories and paradigms of knowledge and reason.

Yet it turns out, when we look for ourselves at the larger landscape, that it displays a structure similar to the one against which philosophers and their acolytes repeatedly rebel. In the larger as well as in the lesser examples there is cause for weighing one consideration with another. A person's faith that evil must at last be overcome may rest on a conviction wide and deep enough to serve as a premise for what is itself a profound and far-ranging belief. A faithful believer in a religion does not typically assert purely dogmatic doctrines but argues from one belief to another as reasoners do in other spheres.

For this reason, a believer must pay careful attention to the logical order to be recognized in or imposed on the various doctrines that he propounds or defends. A good example is provided by the place or places typically occupied, in a wider religious context, by the concept of miracle. One apologist may argue from the occurrence of miracles to a belief in an almighty power capable of bringing about such wondrous changes in the physical order. Another may argue from an initial belief in the almightiness of God to the possibility of miraculous occurrences. Unfortunately, it may also happen that one and the same thinker uses both inferences at different times—and not always at mutually very distant times.

Whatever the sources of our various beliefs, and not only of our religious beliefs, we need invariably to look to the consistency of one belief with another, and to the coherence of what we are willing to recognize as our overall set of beliefs. This is a requirement for our qualifying as rational beings, one that applies across the whole range of our knowledge and understanding. Edmund Gosse's father knew that the different logical origins of his geological knowledge and of his scriptural knowledge did not absolve him from his responsibility for achieving consistency by some adjustment or reinterpretation between his belief that the earth and the whole firmament were created in 4004 BC and his knowledge that geological facts appeared to require an immeasurably earlier date. (See Gosse 1935: ch. 5.)

Others have shown a lesser regard for logical discipline when they have spoken of *kinds* of truth in a way that implies too great an independence of one mode of truth from another. The fact that one belief is theological and another is geological does not mean that we may with philosophical impunity believe them both in spite of their being mutually contradictory. It will not do to say that a miracle story is theologically true while remaining physically or historically false.

All this is preliminary to what I mainly wish to consider; my central concern is with the seductive power of the great dichotomies to lure us into theoretical confusion about matters whose daily conduct presents us with little or no difficulty until we self-consciously reflect upon them. When we grandiloquently speak of Reason as opposed to Faith, it is easy to think that everything to do with reason is on one side, and everything to do with faith is on the other side, of a gulf too wide for anything or any person to cross from one side to the other. It appears to follow that there can be no intellectual component in faith, and so that it is impossible for the articles of a faith to rest upon any grounds or reasons. But if grounds or reasons are exhausted before we reach the beginnings of faith, then the affirmation of an article of faith will necessarily be *arbitrary*—a matter of a *choice* made upon no *basis*. Let us consider a number of conceptions—in my view misconceptions— and their authors or proponents. They may respectively be called *fideism*, *voluntarism* and *existentialism*.

The fideist holds that the reason cannot determine any of the central questions of theology. Every supposed reason in favour of a religious belief is balanced by a countervailing reason against it, leaving us with a scepticism—'Pyrrhonism'—as the only resort for the understanding. If we are willing to commit ourselves to Pascal's wager (Pascal 1966: *Pensée* 418; see also *Pensée* 423), or to adopt any religious position or posture, we do so by exercising an untrammelled choice. The fideist may speak, like Pascal, of 'the heart's reasons that reason is unac- quainted with', but there is likely to be conscious paradox in that formulation; his deliberate theory of the matter is that we are not relying on any grounds or reasons when we subscribe to belief or unbelief. We are *entitled* to affirm a belief because there is no obstacle to doing so, not because there is any ground for doing so.[1]

The notion of entitlement is again prominent in William James's 'will to believe'. We have the right to exercise *options* between doctrines none of which are ruled out by reason. Our 'passional and volitional nature' co-operates with but goes beyond the intellect that judges. Our passions and sentiments 'do actually, and may lawfully' influence us to choose between conflicting beliefs. James regards the exercise of such options as a *creative* process, in which we may *bring about* the truth of what we are choosing to believe. In James's treatment of this notion there is endemic confusion, which may adequately for our present purpose be brought out by his example of the passengers on a train beset by bandits:

> A social organism of any sort whatever, large or small, is what it is because each member proceeds to his own duty with a trust that the other members will simultaneously do theirs. Wherever a desired result is achieved by the co-operation of many independent persons, its existence as a fact is a pure consequence of the precursive faith in one another of those immediately concerned. A government, an army, a commercial system, a ship, a college, an athletic team, all exist on this condition, without which not only is nothing achieved, but nothing is even attempted. A whole train of passengers (individually brave enough) will be looted by a few highwaymen, simply because the latter can count on one another, while each passenger fears that if he makes a movement of resistance, he will be shot before any one else backs him up. If we believed that the whole car-full would rise at once with us, we should each severally rise, and train-robbing would never even be attempted. There are, then, cases where a fact cannot come at all unless a preliminary faith exists in its coming. *And where faith in a fact can help create the fact*, that would be an insane logic which should say that faith running ahead of scientific evidence is the 'lowest kind of immorality' into which a thinking being can fall. Yet such is the logic by which our scientific absolutists pretend to regulate our lives! (James 1956: 24–5)

James here confuses a belief in the sense of *what is believed* with belief in the sense of the *believing* of what is believed, considered as a psychological fact. In his example of the train, the fact that a number of

[1] I am grateful to Martin Warner and to Mary Bambrough for their comments on an earlier version of this paragraph. They have saved me from some at least of my misunderstandings of Pascal.

people believe that others will join them in resistance is a causal influence over subsequent events, in the way that confidence in a cricketer or golfer may improve a stroke. It is only in this causal way that 'faith in a fact' can help to create a fact.

Sartre is more like the text-book fideist than is always recognized. Like the fideist, Sartre asks us to 'choose, that is to say invent', when we find, as we typically shall, that our ethical, religious, political and philosophical perplexities are not resoluble by reason. Again, in his famous example of the young man during the resistance, we meet with the idea of an exact balance of the weights of conflicting considerations, authorizing us to choose *without reason*:

> His father was quarrelling with his mother and was also inclined to be a 'collaborator'; his elder brother had been killed in the German offensive of 1940 and this young man, with a sentiment somewhat primitive but generous, burned to avenge him. His mother was living alone with him, deeply afflicted by the semi-treason of his father and by the death of her eldest son, and her one consolation was in this young man. But he, at this moment, had the choice between going to England to join the Free French Forces or of staying near his mother and helping her to live. He fully realized that this woman lived only for him and that his disappearance—or perhaps his death—would plunge her into despair. (Sartre 1948: 35)

It may be unfair to call Sartre's manoeuvre a confidence trick, since it seems possible that he is deceived by it himself. In that case we can only spare him the moral accusation at the cost of accusing him of a simple confusion. It can be brought out in two related but distinct ways. First, by asking the question: 'How does Sartre know that his two columns of conflicting considerations do exactly balance, each therefore cancelling out the other?' Secondly, by confronting Sartre with a case differing from his own only by a small addition or subtraction from his own. The selection or invention of his actual example is based on our ordinary ethical understanding, in which we recognize duties to parents and to a cause or a country. Although Sartre is explicitly denying that there is such a thing as moral knowledge or understanding, he is implicitly using a voluminous amount of such understanding. Unless he knew that the various considerations had weight, each in one direction or the other, he could not know, as he claims to, that the weights on the two sides are equal. But when he does claim to know all this, he loses any ground he might have thought he had for his assumption that *every* moral claim is between mutually exclusive alternatives in which there is exactly as much reason on one side as on the other. And this is easily shown; for *if* the two sets of considerations do exactly balance, then we need only to add another brother to the family, or take away the father's

Renford Bambrough

treachery to his country and his family, to produce a case in which, on Sartre's own terms, the conclusion is unavoidable that the resulting new case is one in which we *do* know how to respond. And Sartre was already showing an implicit grasp of this objection when he unreflectingly excluded from consideration any number of alternative options that he does not even mention: such as having the young man opt out of all his responsibilities at once by deciding to spend the rest of the war in South America and returning only when things at home (in two senses) have become more comfortable. Sartre's philosophy is even more voluntarist, or *arbitrarian*, than James's 'will to believe'.

Though we constantly forget them these thoughts are not new or unrecognized. Here is a passage from Anthony Kenny's *Faith and Reason*:

> The special nature of the belief that is faith is that it is a belief in something as revealed by God; belief in a proposition on the word of God. Faith, thus defined, is a correlate of revelation; for faith to be possible it must be possible to identify something as the word of God. . . .
>
> Equally, there were many different forms in which the revelation might be made, different channels by which it reached the human race from God—perhaps through Moses or the prophets, perhaps through Christ, or the Bible, or the Church, or even in an enlightenment of the individual conscience. What was common to all these different cases was that the believer's faith was belief in certain propositions as having been specially revealed by God. Because the propositions were not demonstrable without appeal to revelation, because they were indeed opaque and might appear repugnant to the unaided human intelligence, faith in these propositions differed from reason. But because the fact of their being revealed could be proved, it was claimed, beyond rational cavil, faith was not in conflict with reason but was a rational state of mind. Faith was a virtue permitting the mind access to truths which would otherwise be beyond its reach. (Kenny 1983: 69–70)

Basil Mitchell, in *The Justification of Religious Belief*, testifies to the same effect:

> It may still be objected that this familiar opposition between faith and reason presupposes that faith is not itself based on reasons. For if it were, there could be no conflict. The man of faith would persevere in his faith only so long as it remained on balance more likely than not that he would turn out to be right in the end. Only if he persisted beyond that point would it be proper to talk of a conflict between faith and reason.
>
> This objection would stand if men could be supposed always to

have full and explicit understanding of the rational basis of their beliefs and to be able to survey at any time the entire state of the question. But this, as we have seen, is rarely, if ever, the case. The individual does not see everything, nor can he always see clearly what he does see; nor is his judgment unaffected by confused emotions and uncertain purposes. It is in this characteristically human predicament that faith belongs. There would be no need for faith in a world where men had no tendency to lose heart and where circumstances were always clear, stable and unambiguous; and faith would not be a virtue unless it were both difficult and necessary for men to pursue a steady course in the face of dangers, doubts and frustrations. In this situation faith, even when it is in fact reasonable, must often operate in the individual's life as a substitute for reason rather than as a straightforward expression of it. And it must often appear to him that reason is at odds with it, the more especially as 'reason' is readily identified with what can be clearly stated and easily recognized or even with what is currently fashionable or commonly accepted. (Mitchell 1973: 138)

When we return to the scale suggested by the capital letters and the scope of the title of this symposium, we are again threatened by the treachery of the singular, but are now better equipped to fend off the danger. We feel when speaking of Faith and Reason that there must be a pure and sharp distinction, one that puts all the reason on one side of the conjunction and all the non-reason on the other. The non-reason may be will, or faith, or existential choice. It is a short step further to *un*reason, to a state of things in which we pluck our reasons from the air, not being oriented by any star for our guidance. But where there is no such orientation there is no intelligible question either. If we purport to be asking or answering a question all the same we deceive ourselves, and there is no truth in us. Aristotle's view that deliberation is about means not ends will help me to explain what I have in mind here. I can only be deliberating, weighing up the pros and cons, if there are identifiable pros and cons, considerations and factors which evidently point in one of the directions in which the decision is to be reached by the process of deliberation. We have seen that even Sartre implicitly recognizes and expresses an understanding of how the land lies about the dilemma of his young pupil. The distinctions between deliberation and investigation, decision and discovery, choosing and believing make no difference to the present point. There is no faith where we are conscious of being in possession of conclusive argument or evidence, but there is also no faith where there is nothing at all that counts as evidence or argument in favour of the conclusion in which we have faith. The emptying of all reason and evidence out of the willing or

31

choosing or intuition or belief leads to total arbitrariness in which anything whatsoever can be declared as the result. In these circumstances nothing can count as a response or reaction to the world or to any thing or state of affairs within it. It is hardly surprising that the practice of many philosophers is better than their theory, since their theory makes all understanding impossible to us, and to them.

Reason and Faith—II

ROGER TRIGG

I

The categories of reason and faith are often contrasted. When reason gives out, we are told that we have to rely on faith. Such exhortations are made particularly in the context of religion. When for instance, we face some personal tragedy which may well seem inexplicable, we are told that faith can help us through it. Very often faith is referred to in a vacuum. Presumably faith in God is usually meant, but all too often God drops out of the picture, and it seems that all we need is faith, not faith in anything or anyone, but just faith. We are thus encouraged to add what seems to be a magic ingredient to our lives, which can transform everything. Perhaps at the back of such thinking lies some Calvinist notion of the corrupt character of human reason. As a result it may seem that we cannot rely on our judgment, which is the product of the fallen and sinful nature of humanity. Instead we must depend on 'faith' which may, or may not, be given us by the grace of God.

It is in this context that Renford Bambrough's resistance to a sharp dichotomy between faith and reason is especially valuable. He says: 'The simple idea is that faith is itself a mode of reason. This means that there cannot be a sharp distinction between reason and faith'. This must be right, as free-floating faith is not faith at all. If I have faith, it must as a matter of logic be in someone or something. The notion of trust is analogous—I cannot trust without having a particular object in view. I must trust someone or something. To quote one of Bambrough's examples, I can have trust in the Forth Road Bridge. Such trust may be misplaced. If the bridge has just been blown up by terrorists and no longer exists, my trust in it will not get me very far. Similarly, even if it is still there, it may have been structurally weakened and again my trust in it is not well-grounded. In so far as I do trust it, however, I believe that it is there to be crossed, and that it will enable me to cross safely.

Faith has similar features. Whatever I have faith in must exist for my faith to be justified. Having the attitude will not get me across a bridge that has just collapsed, and similarly my faith in my doctor depends crucially on his existence. That may seem silly, but if he has died suddenly this morning, my continuing faith in him as a source of future guidance is not well grounded. Faith involves more than this. I must regard the object of my faith as reliable and worthy of trust. A weakened bridge, or a doctor who is in fact a charlatan, are not proper objects for such faith. As a consequence, reason can well be used to undermine someone's faith. Once I have told you of the death of your doctor or given a chronicle of his misdeeds, your faith will soon vanish if you are not irrational. In this respect, faith is no different from some other categories which are often contrasted with reason. For instance, emotions are not generally free-floating, but typically need an object. I am never simply afraid. I must be afraid of something (or somebody). Similarly I am never angry, without being angry at something. Otherwise, how do I know that my attitude is one of anger, and not something else? Emotions involve thoughts of objects and are defined by the kind of view we take of the object. They become neurotic and irrational precisely at the point when they persist, even though we know the object does not exist, or that our attitude to it is inappropriate. I can be afraid of the man next door even though the house is empty. If my fear persists even when I am told that it is empty, there is something wrong with me. Panic because of a mouse, even a real one, can quickly become irrational. Our reason has to be involved in all our beliefs about the world and in our reactions to it. How else can we continue to live in the world, and cope with reality, if we are not able to adjust our responses, even our emotional ones, so that they are appropriate to the circumstances we are in?

In small things as well as great, we must know what we can continue to trust. We must be prepared to change our attitudes and hence our actions, once we see that our beliefs are wrong. It cannot be an arbitrary matter what we trust or put our faith in. People who have faith in dangerous bridges are liable to get wet. Similarly it is not a good idea to put our faith in someone who will betray us. Faith requires an object, which should, if possible, conform in fact to our beliefs about it. Yet there is always the possibility that we put our faith in what is really an illusion. We can believe that someone is trustworthy when there is no-one there to trust in the first place. In philosophical jargon, intentional objects (the targets of our thoughts) need not exist. When they do not, our fear or anger, or even our faith, can remain real enough. Because, though, they are totally misdirected, they are groundless. For anyone who desires to be rational, and to live in the world as it is, as opposed to the way we imagine it to be, it is vitally important that we discover where the truth lies. Are we right to be angry or afraid? Are we justified in the faith we profess? The answers to these questions crucially depend on the existence and character of the objects concerned. In each case, we have to differentiate between subject and object, between the person possessing faith and the object of faith. In the case of religious faith, it is typically faith in God, so that it can only be justified if there is a God who possesses the character imputed to Him. Faith implies belief that there is an appropriate object for the faith. There is an inescapable propositional element in any commitment. (See Trigg 1973.)

The distinction between the subject and object of faith may seem innocuous, but it follows, if it is taken seriously, that we should hold a realist view of religious faith. Realism holds that what reality is like and how we conceive it are always separate questions (see Trigg 1989). The nature of faith depends above all on the possible independent existence of what we have faith in. Faith cannot be a mere decision to live a certain kind of life, nor is it an arbitrary commitment. It must involve a specific belief about its object. Whether our faith is justified or not depends on whether that belief is true. It certainly may not be. The object of faith may not be as we conceive it to be, to the extent of not even existing. This demonstrates the simple distinction between our thoughts and what our thoughts are about, or the dichotomy between the subject and object of belief. This distinction between subject and object may appear to be merely a grammatical one, reflecting the structure of our language. Yet as in all cases of belief and knowledge, there must be no confusion between the fact of belief and its content, between the person believing, and what is believed. Faith can be real enough in its influence even when it is totally misplaced. We can begin to cross a bridge even though it is not going to bear our weight. How the world is is not necessarily how we think it is. The world, and the individual self taking up an attitude to it, exists each in its own right. The person with faith in God exemplifies this. The subject of faith possesses it, but the faith is directed at something that must be totally independent. That is why we always have to face the question whether the God who is trusted even exists.

II

This all may seem to be labouring an obvious point, but in fact it is something which would be vehemently denied by many contemporary philosophers. The idea that 'reality' or 'the world' has an intrinsic nature, which we as subjects of beliefs attempt to represent, is explicitly rejected. Many separate currents of philosophy combine to overwhelm the simple distinction between subject and object. Everything, we are told, is the contingent creation of language. The world, our beliefs, and even ourselves are all linguistic creations. The influence of Nietzsche, and more recently the later Wittgenstein, is obvious in all this, but there are other strands, such as American pragmatism, to reckon with as well. Richard Rorty exemplifies an approach which combines all these

Roger Trigg

strands, and, perhaps significantly, explicitly links the traditional realist position with a theistic outlook. He says, for example: 'The very idea that the world or the self has an intrinsic nature—one which the physicist or the poet may have glimpsed—is a remnant of the idea that the world is a divine creation, the work of someone who had something in mind, who Himself spoke some language in which He described His own project.' (Rorty 1989: 21)

Rorty denies that there is any sense in the view that the world does have such an intrinsic nature. He does not consider that some vocabularies are better than others at representing the world. He then alleges that 'to drop the idea of languages as representations . . . would be to de-divinize the world.' Rorty claims to find a trend away from the need humans once felt 'to worship something which lay beyond the visible world'. He alleges that with the growth of science, we substituted a love of Truth for the love of God, and then later a romantic love of ourselves for the pursuit of science. Contemporary thought, emanating from such people as Nietzsche and Freud, suggests, according to Rorty, 'that we try to get to the point where we no longer worship *anything*, where we treat *nothing* as a quasi divinity, where we treat *everything*—our language, our conscience, our community—as a product of time and chance' (22).

Rorty attacks the view that there could be One Right Description, and says that we must simply aim 'at an expanding repertoire of alternative descriptions'. This, he believes, is possible 'only to the extent that both the world and the self have been de-divinized'. (Rorty 1989: 39–40) There is thus no one real world, any more than we are substantial selves confronting it. The solidity of the contrast between subject and object is destroyed. There can be no place for any metaphysical conception of a reality possibly transcending our belief and our language. We are left with different sets of apparent descriptions, none of which can claim any greater validity than any other. We must, Rorty says, drop 'the image of a preestablished harmony between the human subject and the object of knowledge' (67). It is significant that it is not just the distinction between subject and object which is thereby undermined. Since the traditional picture suggests that the relation between the two is ideally a rational one, the whole function of reason is put into question. No longer can we be understood as reasoning towards a true conclusion. Reason is revealed as an illusion. Rorty explicitly denies any distinction between it and passion. He does this, too, not to suggest that passion can have a rational element, but to deny any separate role for reason. Mentioning Freud, he denies that we should split persons up in this way, though Freud's own classification of ego, super-ego and id might suggest a continuing distinction.

Rorty rules out any conception of the 'absolute validity' of beliefs, and explicitly connects it with 'the assumption of a self which divides fairly neatly into the part it shares with the divine and the part it shares with the animals' (Rorty 1989: 47). Thus concepts of truth and validity are linked with the possibility of reason, which in turn is linked with the existence of the divine. All are denied. Yet many would question this assumption that there can be no role for a dispassionate, free-floating reason without God. Indeed such a characterization of reason is often attributed to the Enlightenment which was often self-consciously athe-istic. Certainly the idea that one can conclude rationally that there is no God would not seem to be self-contradictory. Yet if reason can only be understood as a spark of the divine, it would in effect be undermining itself by arguing for atheism. Perhaps, in a sense, this has consciously happened in the development of the kind of relativist, post-modernist view put forward by Rorty. He is clearly arguing that without divine foundations to rest on, we must rule out the very idea of a reason that can transcend all vocabularies and conceptual frameworks and arrive in some mysterious way at objective truth. The obvious rejoinder must be that if Rorty purports to be offering anything resembling a philosophi-cal argument for the impossibility of rationality, he must himself be appealing to the very rationality he is questioning.

Philosophers, such as Hilary Putnam, often talk of the impossibility of a God's eye view of the world, that is of the impossibility of giving a unique, correct description of the way things are. The very idea of truth seems to recede into the distance especially when the existence of an omniscient God is not assumed. We can, it seems, only speak from our standpoint with the interpretation of whatever form of life we belong to. Realism is thus linked to a theism that is briskly ruled out. Every-thing becomes anthropocentric or, worse, relative to the standards of whatever community we happen to owe allegiance to. Reason is impos-sible without the resources of language, it is alleged, and all languages are historical products, rooted in the contingencies of particular times and places. Thus the idea of any faith stretching out towards some metaphysical reality cannot be taken seriously. Our beliefs cannot transcend themselves, so that the conception of the self as subject reasoning about any kind of object existing independently must be mistaken. Reason, truth, selves and so on are all linguistic creations. Indeed, Don Cupitt (1990: x) says provocatively that 'like us, God is made only of words.' It seems that there can be no supra-historical ground of reasoning. We must be content with what Rorty (1989: 68) terms a 'historical narrative' of the ground of our customs and institutions.

If all this is philosophical argument, rather than empty rhetoric, it certainly succeeds in destroying itself spectacularly. As has already been indicated, an argument that decries the possibility of argument cannot be very persuasive. The aim of so much 'post-modernist' philosophy seems to be to undermine the very possibility of reason and hence of philosophy. The result is a relativism that forces us to be satisfied with the assumptions of our own society, however that is defined. A lurking shadow threatens even more. We may be confronted with a crippling nihilism that takes away from us even the comfortable assumptions we at present have. However that may be, an intriguing aspect of Rorty's position is the way he explicitly links reason, truth and reality on the one hand with the idea of God. Since atheism would become self-contradictory it must be too quick to conclude that realism implies theism. Rorty's association of the two, and his view of reason as associated with the divine, may carry a different implication. Theism must, it may be suggested, entail realism, and give an objective grounding for the human exercise of reason. Even an idealist, such as Bishop Berkeley, accepted the independent reality of God, by whom everything is perceived. God was for him the guarantor of truth, as He must be in any theistic system. He provides the grounding for our reasoning, and gives us the right to assume that our reasoning is not the mere accidental product of time and place. However limited our understanding, if there is a God, we can be provided with the assurance that rationality is no illusion.

Human fallibility, or sin, may warp our judgments, but there must always be the prior question whether, even in principle, there is anything to reason about. Is our reason a mere function of the kind of language we happen to speak or, alternatively, is our language the vehicle for a rationality that can transcend the undoubted constraints put upon us by our historical circumstances? The picture of a rationality that can grasp, however partially, what is true about the world and our place in it, depends on a picture of objective truth which is guaranteed by theism. The problem as to how we can break out of the shackles put on us by our human concepts is lessened if we can know that there is a God who is the goal of our intellectual striving and who, Himself, by his perfect knowledge, sets the standard at which we should aim. There is, however, a problem. The transcendent reality of the objects of knowledge, as demanded by realism, is no different in metaphysical status from the transcendent reality of God. Grounding the former in the latter does not carry the matter much farther forward, it may be thought. *If* there is a God, then He is the guarantor of the possibility of knowledge. How, though, can we know that there is a God, or even understand the notion of His independent existence? One answer sometimes given is that we can only do so by His intervention or revelation. This viewpoint, while stressing the indissoluble link between faith and reason might indicate the priority of faith. However that may be, the point at issue is that if theism is true, some form of metaphysical realism seems to follow. The very idea that there is a God, who exists independently of human conceptions lies at the very heart of religious faith. It is also the supreme example of a realist position.

III

The implicit connection with theism may make many philosophers frightened of metaphysical realism. There is a lurking suspicion even when it is pointed out that all ontological claims, including atheism, materialism and physicalism, are claims about the nature of objective reality. It seems as if the related ideas of reason and truth can all too easily be talked of as if they have gained capital letters, and are the tools of some theistic enterprise. Such worries seem widespread, and it is all the more surprising to find an apparently Christian thinker accept much of Rorty's position and deny that Christianity itself needs any sort of realist position. Don Cupitt says: 'I agree with Rorty that we . . . now find ourselves having to live without old-style metaphysical or theological underpinning for our final vocabulary. Yes: for me too everything is contingent, a product of history and open to re-assessment'. (Cupitt 1990: 15–16)

Cupitt talks of 'our post-modern universe made only of contingencies, relativities and interpretation.' His position is aggressively and explicitly anti-realist, stressing the dependency of all our thought on our language, together with the transient nature of our language. According to him, whatever we understand by God, there is certainly no deity existing independently of the language of human beings. Whatever religion is, it cannot be the worship of a transcendent Being. This, he readily recognizes, has implications for the possibility of reason and knowledge. He writes: 'Our disputes are interminable because there isn't an eternal umpire. That is, there isn't a fixed intelligible reality out there, quite independent of our various angles upon it, and available to serve as an impartial umpire between us. . . . We do not have and we could not have access to any extra-linguistic and extra-human meanings and truths.' (Cupitt 1990: 20)

As a result, Cupitt is strongly opposed to any metaphysical realism, which holds that 'there is an objective, intelligible order out there and independent of our discourse' (44). We cannot hold to any grand idea of Truth, because, says Cupitt, 'truth is human, socially produced, historically-developed, plural and changing'. Questions about reality become transmuted into questions about language, and since language is always in flux it cannot conceive of any Final Truth. Cupitt maintains that 'the world is an argument that never gets settled' (60). Indeed, in truly relativist fashion, he says flatly at one point that 'people of different periods live in different worlds' (105). As with all such positions, there is considerable danger of incoherence. Cupitt appears to be making a claim about what is the case. He seems to think that he lives in a world in which it is true that people of different periods live in different ones. It is difficult to make any assertion at all without laying some claim to what is objectively so. His intention, however, is clear. He seeks to dissolve the objective side of the subject-object relationship. Instead of being a target for our thoughts and beliefs, it becomes, at best, the mere shadow cast by them.

The paradox is that, at the same time, no room is left for the subject. This is perhaps hardly surprising as it will be alleged that the idea of a substantial self reaching out into the world, in order to obtain knowledge, is shot through with metaphysics. Such a self is typically the possessor of a reason that precedes language and transcends the society of which it is a member. Instead of being a creation of time and place, it would be able to rise above the constraints and barriers of its contingent circumstances. As Cupitt himself recognizes, this idea of the self goes with a refusal to identify thought and language, since that is immediately to limit the possibilities of our understanding. Cupitt sees that this picture of the self is of someone made in the image of God, who could in a finite way think God's thoughts after Him. He says: 'The self and God transcended human language *together*.' (165) Thus attacks on the metaphysical self often go hand in hand with attacks on the possibility of a transcendent God (see Trigg 1988a: 277ff). Both are regarded as metaphysical constructs, which can be dispensed with under the influence of Nietzsche. The whole picture is rejected of a separately existing subject using reason to grasp something of the truth of a self-subsistent object.

Cupitt makes his position clear when he writes: 'The human subject as a metaphysical subject, a rational soul more-or-less prior to and independent of history and the body, was already in dire trouble even before Darwin, but in William James and Nietzsche it clearly disappears. With it go unchanging Reason and Truth out-there.' (Cupitt 1990: 188) The repudiation of the possibility of any reasoning towards any truth, understood objectively, can, and perhaps must, result in a devastating conclusion. Cupitt certainly accepts that now 'we are nihilists'. He amplifies this by explaining that 'nihilism means the death of God followed by the death of Man; it means the end of metaphysics followed by the end of ideology' (193). Thus Cupitt not only denies the existence of God, at least as traditionally understood. He also sweeps aside any idea of ourselves as rational, autonomous subjects. In addition, he denies the possibility of such a thing as human nature, existing through different epochs, and perhaps in some measure explaining the characteristics of human society.

Yet the question must be faced how far any form of religious faith can survive such an onslaught on the possibility of reason. As we have seen, the very idea of faith presupposes the dichotomy between subject and object. Once, though, it is conceded that what we have beliefs about may possess an independent existence, metaphysics, as the study of that reality, becomes essential. Some argue that Christianity does not need any metaphysical underpinning. A reliance on reason seems very suspect to some who insist on the predominant role of faith. Indeed it is sometimes made to seem a commonplace that the God of the philosophers has little to do with the God of faith. Some may ask what true religion has to do with clever intellectual theories. It should be apparent, however that this is a false choice. We need our reason to show us what it is we have faith in. Metaphysics is not an alternative to faith. It gives faith its rational grounding.

Revealed religion may seem to have little need for human reasoning. When faith is understood as a gift from God it may even seem presumptuous to think that we can reason about God's existence, as if He were part of the furniture of the world or, worse, the conclusion of a theorem which had to be proved. Certainly the history of Christian theology has seen a continued tug-of-war between the categories of faith and reason. At one extreme, Enlightenment conceptions have encouraged the idea of human reason as sovereign and in control of our destiny. Such conceptions, often linked with the development of the physical sciences, were perhaps responsible for the French Revolution, which encouraged some activities which were far from rational. On the other hand, an idea that faith can somehow appear without the aid of reason is equally dangerous. Because our faith is always faith in something, we can only retain the language of faith by keeping to the idea of a relationship between subject and object. However much we may wish to distance ourselves from the Enlightenment conception of autonomous reason, we dare not uphold the idea of faith as an alternative to rationality. Faith without reason is blind. It is faith in nothing. We must have a conception of what, or whom, we trust, if faith is to have any meaning.

Religious 'faith' can perhaps be shorthand for describing a particular aesthetic outlook, or moral viewpoint. It can even degenerate into an ephemeral political programme. Perhaps Cupitt exemplifies something of this when he surprisingly attacks the philosophical doctrine of realism as 'cosmic Toryism' (Cupitt 1990: 54). Faith in such contexts cannot be faith as it is generally understood. Whatever the aesthetic, moral and political implications of religious faith, and Christian faith in particular, it must essentially involve belief in God. There may be room

Roger Trigg

for discussion as to what is meant by 'God', but it is absolutely necessary that there is a distinction between the person with faith and the object of faith. My faith in God must involve trust in someone beyond myself. Our understanding of the nature of God may well change. The possibility of faith is dissolved, however, if we accept that there is nothing objective to trust. This cannot be a question about the use of language, but is a deep fact about ourselves and our relationship with the world.

Cupitt attacks the notion of a self with as much vigour as he denies the existence of an objective God. Yet faith implies a subject as well as an object. We may sometimes reify faith and trust it as if it were itself a substantial entity. Sometimes 'faith' appears to mean a body of belief. At root, however, just as there is no such thing as hope, but only people who hope for something, so there is no faith, but only people who have faith in something. Faith reaches beyond what is properly demonstrable, and there must always be an element of uncertainty in it, however assured we are of its truth. Faith is not knowledge, however much it aspires to be. It is always vulnerable and if, as we have seen, our reason shows us that it is in some way mistaken, we have to give it up. We can make no greater error than to have faith in something that does not exist. Cupitt has a blanket argument against the possibility of conceiving of any objective reality independent of language. His apparent atheism and nihilism is the result of his explicit stand against realism. His wholesale attack on metaphysics cannot, though, soften the impact of his onslaught on the nature of Christian faith. Without the possibility of an independently existing God, we can have no faith, if we are to use our reason.

As rational thinkers we must aim at times to transcend the constraints of our social environment. Language is the tool of our thinking and not its prison. The human intellect is restless and always attempts to grasp something of its place in the scheme of things. Sometimes we try to rise above the evidence of our senses, and attempt to understand the physical world in its entirety and what if anything lies beyond it. Above all, we have to be motivated in our reasoning and in whatever faith we possess by the belief that there is a truth to be discovered and that, therefore, there is a distinction between the way things are and the way they are not. This realist conception, derided by self-styled 'postmodernists' lies at the root of all human intellectual activity. Without it, philosophy itself has no point. Rorty comments that 'to say, with Nietzsche, that God is dead, is to say that we serve no higher purposes' (1989: 20). Rorty is saying that there can be no distinction, ultimately, between truth and falsity, light and darkness. All we can have is a picture of successive views, aimlessly following each other through the generations. Yet what motivates those like Rorty and Cupitt who attack all forms of traditional metaphysics? Presumably they believe that those who have faith in a transcendent Being are simply mistaken. An anti-realist appears to be offering arguments against realism. The confrontation between realists and anti-realists, at least in the field of religion, must surely at some level involve questions of truth. The advocacy of anti-realism itself masquerades as a parade of reason. If it does not provide us with rational arguments, there can be no grounds for taking it seriously. The possibility of the exercise of reason in the pursuit of truth is not a metaphysical illusion. It is not even an optional extra. The meaningful use of language and its deployment in the arts of persuasion depends on it. Without a distinction between truth and falsity there can be no constraint on what we say or any purpose in saying it. Language collapses. There is no way through nihilism.

Faith can persist so long as it is believed that its object is real, but it logically cannot survive an acceptance of its unreality. It is irrelevant whether this arises only in the particular case, or stems from a global view about reality. We cannot as persons relate to the world, unless we see a difference between ourselves as subjects and the objects with which we hope to interact. The post-modernist critique of traditional ways of thinking may appear to function at an abstract, philosophical level. In a way it does, even though it paradoxically denies philosophy any function. It also has a catastrophic impact on the possibility of all reason and all faith, within religion and outside it. It demolishes any conception of reality or of the possibility of knowledge. In fact, as a supposedly rational onslaught on the very possibility of rationality, it also destroys itself.

The Logic of Mysticism—I

HERBERT McCABE

This title represents, I suppose, a kind of challenge; for there seems at first sight some incompatibility between the practice of logic and mysticism, a contrast between the rational and the intuitive, the tough minded and the tender-minded. In taking up this challenge, I propose to argue with the help of two thinkers commonly admired for their attention to logic and its rights. I shall refer for the most part to St Thomas Aquinas but with occasional reference to Wittgenstein. Whatever may be said of the latter, it seems to me quite clear that St Thomas was a mystical thinker in that he was centrally concerned with the unknown and, in one sense, ineffable mystery of God and that he devoted a great deal of thought and writing to the problems associated with speaking of what is, in this sense, ineffable. I want to argue that in what is sometimes misunderstood as his dryly rational approach, even in his arguments for the existence of God, he is in fact engaged in, and inviting the reader to be engaged in, a mystical exploration, which is not at all the same thing as a mystical experience. Here the key notion is that of what he refers to as *esse*.

Perhaps I should say right away that for St Thomas we come to see the need for the particular use he has for the word *esse* (which is, after all, only the Latin infinitive of the verb to be) as the result of an argument not as the result of an experience—not even the experience of being convinced by an argument. It is a central thesis of his that we grasp the use of this word not as we grasp other meanings—by what he calls *simplex apprehensio*, the having of a concept or the understanding of a meaning, eg. having learnt and not forgotten the meaning of, say, *'fatwah'*—but as we deploy such concepts in the making of true or false judgments which issue not in meanings but in statements. It is not simply in our capacity to use signs, our ability, for example, to understand words, but in our actual use of them to say what is the case that we have need of and lay hold on the *esse* of things. It is only by analogy that we can speak of the 'concept' of *esse*, we do not have a concept of existence as we have a concept of greenness or prevarication or polar bears.

In order to make sense of this use of *esse* I shall need to begin with our familiar understanding of things existing and not existing. It is generally believed that there are no dodos any more. If, however, the rumour arose that some had survived in the remote interior of Mauritius, an expedition might set forth for these parts to inquire into the matter. Whatever else these explorers brought with them, an essential piece of equipment would be some understanding of what distinguishes dodos from parrots and ptarmigans. They would have to grasp the meaning of the word 'dodo' sufficiently to be able, in that geographical context, to pick out dodos from other things. They would then hope to discover something that fitted their formula: some x, such that x was a dodo. It is in just such a context that the conventional account of what it is to say that something exists is at home. Philosophers have been anxious to point out that when we want to know whether dodos exist we do not go and look at dodos to see whether they have existence or not; we go to see whether there is anything at all that would count as a dodo. It was a point familiar to Aristotle and to medieval thinkers: to ask *an sit?* (whether it is) you have to start with at least some meaning for a word.

Suppose, then, to everyone's surprise, we are successful and we find some dodos. We shall then have answered the question *an sit*. Having done so we shall be able to settle down with them in their proper habitat, and by living amongst them over the years we may come slowly to some *scientia*, some scientific understanding of what is essential to being a dodo, what it takes for it to exist at all, and what is merely adventitious, as eg. living exclusively in Mauritius or looking slightly ridiculous to slightly ridiculous European observers. This will ordinarily involve the elaboration of a new section of language or a jargon. What first struck people about dodos was their apparent foolishness and clumsiness, hence the original Portuguese name '*doudo*', meaning awkward, and the international term '*didus ineptus*'. As we came to understand more clearly the nature of the dodo, its essence or substance, we should probably devise some quite new name to signify this nature. In this way chemists devised the sign H_2O the meaning of which (ie. its relationship to such other signs as HCl, CO_2 etc.) expresses, on the one hand, the essential structure common to such apparently quite diverse objects as those called 'ice', 'water' and 'steam', and, on the other hand, the natural physical relationships of such substances to what used to be called 'muriatic acid' and 'carbonic acid gas'. We should, in fact, try to devise a jargon with a structure of meanings reflecting the actual structures of the physical, chemical, biological world. Thus we should get closer to what an Aristotelian would call a definition expressing the essence of the thing, we would be closer to answering the new question: *quid sit?*—what does it take for such a thing to exist? If, as Aristotle remarked, there is nothing corresponding to our definition, nothing with this essence, then what looks like a definition of the essence is, in fact, nothing more than an explanation of the meaning of a word.

Understanding of what a dodo is would come ordinarily from a lengthy process of observation and experiment, a process I have called 'living with' the object of our study, and for this to take place there obviously have to be such objects. So, to repeat, we start with the common meaning of the name, sufficient for picking out the object in a particular context; we can then answer the question *an sit*, and if we answer that in the affirmative we can go on by investigation to get clearer about *quid sit*. Despite what nominalist philosophers may say, this is what ordinary working scientists such as chemists and botanists think they are sometimes engaged in. Our conventional account of what it is to say that tame tigers exist or that yetis do not exist is at home in just this context. Of course not all, in fact rather little, of our rational discourse is like doing chemistry—not even for chemists. One way of understanding our rational discourse concerning God is to see how radically it differs from this.

In seeking to show that we can prove the existence of God, that God's existence is *demonstrabile*, St Thomas faces a technical objection. In a true demonstration, as for example in the theorems of Euclid, we show not merely that something is the case but that it has to be the case. To demonstrate is to produce *scientia*, an understanding of how and why the world is as it is. Anyone may know that sugar, unlike marble, dissolves in water; it takes a physical chemist to show how this has to be the case given the molecular structure of the materials involved. His aim is to demonstrate that because of the nature of sugar, because of his definition of its essence, *of course* it dissolves.

The objector begins by stating that '*medium demonstrationis est quod quid est*', the central link of demonstration is the defined nature. (Thomas Aquinas 1964–81: vol. II, la. 2, 2) Then, he argues, to demonstrate that God exists must be to show that, given the definition of his nature, he has to exist; but since we do not know the definition of his nature, but only what he is not, we cannot have a demonstration that he exists. The objector is arguing that the only demonstration that God exists would have to be something like the Anselmian ontological argument in which the existence of God is thought to follow logically from something about God's nature. St Thomas in reply does not deny that we are ignorant of God's nature, but he points out that answering the question *an sit* is quite other than the kind of demonstration in which you show how some operation or effect has to flow from a thing the definition of whose nature you already know. Trying to find if there are any yetis is quite different from trying to show that sugar has to dissolve in water. We go looking for footprints in the snow and if we find them we argue that, given this evidence, *it has to be the case* that yetis exist; we do not seek to show that *yetis have to* exist, just that they do. We are arguing that an opponent necessarily has to accept the proposition, not that the proposition is a necessary one. In such an argument, then, we start not by knowing what God would be but only from features of the world we do know and which seem to be effects of God. It is our knowledge of these effects and not any knowledge of God's nature that gives us our rules for the use of the word 'God'. So you start by claiming that certain phenomena are effects, ie. must have a cause. Not everything that is the case does have a cause: the stars in the night sky are arranged, it is alleged, in patterns reminiscent of various Greek gods and heroes, but it would be very odd to look for some power whose characteristic activity was the cause of this. But St Thomas, as is well-known, thought that certain phenomena such as real change from mere potentiality to actuality, and the power of certain things to effect such change, did demand causal explanation. So he answers his objector here:

> When we argue from effect to cause, the effect will take the place of the definition of the cause in the proof that the cause exists; and this is especially so if the cause is God. For when proving anything to exist the central link is not what that thing is (we cannot even ask what it is (*quid est*) until we know that it exists (*an est*)) but rather what we are using the name of the thing to mean. Now when demonstrating from effects that God exists, we are able to use as link what the word 'God' means, for, as we shall see, the names of God are derived from these effects. (Thomas Aquinas 1964–81: vol. II, la. 2, 2 ad 2)

In this reply, as it seems to me, St Thomas is, as so often, simply saying enough to answer an objection; not, as it were, showing his whole hand. We should in fact be misled if we took it that his arguments for the existence of God start from a 'nominal definition' of God, as though he said: 'This is what people use the word "God" to mean, this is how we can at least pick out God from other things, now let us see if there is one.' It is, to my mind, of the greatest importance that his arguments *end* with, but certainly do not *begin* with: 'and this is what people call "God"'. The arguments do not presuppose any view of the nature of God, they simply begin with philosophical puzzles arising from features of the world that we understand and take us to what we do not understand. They start with questions we can answer and lead us to a question we cannot answer. St Thomas would accept Wittgenstein's statement: 'A question [can exist] only where there is an answer' (*Tractatus*: 6.51), but in this case we know that we cannot give the answer for that would be to know God's nature which is beyond the margins of our ways of grasping meanings. But of this more in a moment.

We need to take a brief look now at the kind of argument St Thomas has in mind. We may begin by noticing that there is some parallel between dependence in causality and dependence in information; indeed the latter is a particular case of the former. Some of the things I know I know because I am a witness to them, but most of what I know (and nearly all the interesting things) I do not know in that way but by hearsay. If I am to know by hearsay it is not, of course, sufficient merely to have been told. I must have been told by one who is reliable, and her reliability must be due either to her being herself a witness or else to her having had, in her turn, a reliable informant, and so on. Unless hearsay is finally anchored, as it were, in what is not hearsay but witness, there can be no reliable hearsay, only baseless rumour. I can really know what I am told only if there is or was someone who knows or knew without being told. Faith, which 'comes by hearing', has to depend on somebody's knowing.

This argument you will perhaps recognize as having the same logical structure as the one St Thomas sketches as the second of his Five Ways. If there are things that have to be brought from potentiality to existence by the power of another thing, there must be one or more things that are not under this condition: that exist actively and are not brought into existence and activity by another. Just as what I am told is only as reliable as the witness who did not need to be told, just as the truth I think I know on hearsay depends totally on the truth of what that witness says, so the existence of anything that has to be brought into existence by another depends totally on the existence and activity of one that does not have to be so brought into existence. Note that in each case the conclusion of the argument is to something that is known *negatively*, to something that does NOT have a dependency of some sort. There is no suggestion of what, positively, such a being might be. All the arguments lead to a power which is not of a kind we understand: to an unknown God. When I repeat what I know by reliable hearsay I am ultimately being the mouthpiece of the original reliable witness. In the same way every creature that exercises its power to bring things or features of things into being is ultimately the instrument of the power which is not the instrument of anything.

It seems (though I shall want to qualify this later in the case of God) that nothing exists except by being something, some kind of thing. What exists does so by having a particular form. 'No entity without identity' as Quine used to say; '*forma dat esse*' as St Thomas used to say. When a cause brings an effect into being it does so by providing the form by which this effect is and has its particular essence—though in the case of caused features of things (which, as St Thomas says, rather *insunt* than *sunt*) we should perhaps speak of an 'inessence'. A cause in nature does this by giving a new form to what previously existed by another form but was capable of losing this (perishing or changing) and being given a new one. When I was brought into existence by my parents they trans-formed material things of various kinds, eg. the food they had eaten, the genes they had inherited, into a material thing of a new kind, existing by a new *human* form we call a human *life*. Before I existed there was already a natural world of material things that were potentially of my kind—not in the sense that they themselves had the power to become human, but simply in the sense that they could be made into, trans-formed into, a human being; and there were other material things with the power to effect this trans-formation. Before I existed there was already a natural world with a me-shaped hole in it waiting to be filled by the active power of a cause. Now natural causality is like hearsay: trans-formation is a genuine source of existence, as hearsay is a genuine source of truth. The possibility of receiving existence from a merely trans-forming cause (like the possibility of receiving truth from mere hearsay) depends on anchorage in a being which is more than a trans-forming cause, a being which is the source of existence as the original witness is the source of a truth. Such a being would not make by the trans-forming of what already has another form, a making 'out of' what already exists. Its bringing into existence must take place without the attendance of a background world, without any background at all, not even empty space.

Natural causes, operating as trans-formers, provide the answer to the question: Why did these things come to exist instead of those others that used to exist or instead of those others that might have existed? Answer: Because they were brought about by this cause that operates in this particular way because of its own particular form. (Explanation by appeal to the specific causal powers of things within the world—things with their own special natures—is the characteristically Aristotelian alternative to the Platonic appeal to participation in the eternal forms.) God, on the other hand, would provide the answer to the question: Why is there anything at all rather than nothing? The object of natural trans-forming causes is the existence of something that has this or that particular form. The object of the divine creative cause is the existence of everything that has existence. I say that God *would* provide the answer to that question (Why is there anything instead of nothing?) because, since we do not know what God is, we do not have an answer to our question.

Natural agents can only have the power to bring things into existence by transformation because they are instruments of God's causality—just as hearsay can only convey truth because it is from the mouthpiece of the original witness. We can certainly say that it is the fire that brings into being the boiling of the water (because that is its nature and natural power); we also say, in a different tone of voice, that God, using the instrumentality of the fire, boils the kettle. Everything that is brought about by natural causes is brought about by God; and there are some things, like human free decisions, that are not brought about by any natural causes but *only* by God.

The artist's colours are arranged in blobs on his palette and his brush moves them and puts them in a new arrangement on the canvas so that a painting is made. In this way the power of the brush to move the paint makes a work of art. But that it makes a work of art is because it is wielded by the artist. In this illustration we can for the artist read *God*, for the paint-brush read the *natural trans-forming cause*, for the new arrangement of the paint read the new *form*, and for the work of art *the new thing* that exists by this form.

We refer to natural trans-forming causes when, given the world, we want to ask scientific questions: Was it the fire that boiled the water or was it the micro-wave? We refer to God when we are asking a more radical question: Why do explanations explain what they do? Why do trans-forming causes bring things into existence?—as we might ask: Why is this hearsay reliable?

Given the natural world, we understand the natures of things by contrast with what they are not. Given the world, we understand what it is for this to exist through its particular form by contrast with what exists by another form. The structuralist is surely right here to insist that meanings consist in oppositions of contraries. This at least seems right when we are allowed to take the world for granted. But suppose we try to understand not simply what it is to exist by this particular form—to see it as the expectable product of this power in the world and not that—but the existence of the world itself. This would be trying to understand the power upon which particular powers depend for their efficacy. If it be true that there has to be such a power, then the world we take for granted must be *granted* in a much richer and more mysterious sense.

It is this gratuitousness of things that St Thomas calls their *esse*: their existence not just over-against the possibility that they might not have been a part of the world (if natural causes had operated differently—which is why the dodos do not exist), but their existence over-against the possibility that there might not have been any world at all. In thinking of the *esse* of things we are trying to think of them not just in relation to their natural causes but in their relation to a creator. If we can simply take the world for granted then within this world to exist is just to be this kind of thing (there is an x such that x is a dodo), for things in the world that come into existence and perish (contingent things) there is a polarity of potential matter and actualising form, but there is no demand for a polarity of essence and existence. It is only when we consider the world as created that we see that even non-contingent, 'necessary beings' (which would not, indeed, depend for their existence and meaning on other natural causes) would have a dependent existence in relation to God. So in all created things beyond the polarity belonging to contingency (based on the distinction of matter and form) there is the polarity of createdness (based on a distinction of essence and existence) which would belong to even 'necessary beings'. Only in the Uncreated is there no potentiality in any sense at all, not even a distinction of essence and existence; only the Uncreated exists without *having* existence. This distinction between contingency with respect to form and dependency with respect to existence is clearly spelled out in St Thomas' Third Way.

Put it this way: you may at some time have a very strong feeling of the gratuity of things, a quasi-religious experience as in nature-mysticism, which seems to contain or lead into a sense of gratitude for there being a world. In the Romantic tradition this was associated with the wilder countryside, especially Cumbria. The sense that we are here under-standing some great truth is, however, vulnerable to recognising the naturalness of nature, a scientific recognition of the complex causes by which the world just had to become the way it is. You may remember the story of the man expatiating on the wonders of Niagara Falls—all those thousands of tons of water cascading down every minute—and his friend who remarked: 'But, after all, what is there to stop it?' It is understandable that Victorian scientific rationalists should have sought to replace such Romantic nature-mysticism with the 'wonders of sci-ence' which seemed less likely to threaten them with metaphysics. 'Wonder' is, however, not part of the vocabulary of science, any more than is 'existence' or 'God' or, indeed, 'science'.

But there remains the wonder that there is science at all, that there is a world of powers and action and new existents. This is not itself one of the wonders of science, and however fascinating the work of physicists investigating the Big Bang it is not relevant to this mystery of gra-tuitousness, the createdness, the *esse* of things.

When I speak of science I am not restricting the term to the mathe-matically governed 'physical sciences'; I mean any and every account of how what happens in the world 'has to happen' (necessarily or naturally or of course). What characterises science in this sense is not necessarily an appeal to mathematics but an appeal to an order of nature, to the essence and character of things such that they act in expectable ways. David Hume, for whose empiricist epistemology knowing was essen-tially a matter of having mental images, denied that things really have powers and tendencies and expectable behaviour, for while you may be able to make a picture of me balancing a billiard cue on my nose, you cannot in the same way make a picture of me being able or likely to perform this feat. However, knowing what things are capable of and likely to do is a large part of understanding what they are; a man who showed no surprise at all at seeing a rabbit chasing a wolf would show that he knew very little about the nature of rabbits and wolves. Our scientific understanding of what goes on around us is rooted in such expectations. But talk of *esse*, the gratuitousness of things, has no place, and ought to have no place, in such natural science.

When Wittgenstein in the *Tractatus* says: 'Not *how* the world is, is the mystical, but *that* it is' (1933: 6.44) it seems to me that he is engaged with the same question as St Thomas is when he speaks of *esse*. As St Thomas distinguishes between the creative act of God (which we do not understand) and natural causality (which we do), between creation and trans-formation, Wittgenstein distinguishes the mystical from 'what can be said' (6.53). Positivist interpretations of the *Tractatus* took this as a cheerful dismissal of all such metaphysical talk, but it now seems to be the general view that this was far from his intention and the unease which is shown (but cannot be said) at the end of the work is an unease with the sharp dichotomy of *either* scientific language *or* silence, an unease which perhaps subsequently bore fruit in his later stress on the multiplicity of language-games.

For St Thomas, then, the *esse* of things turns out to be their createdness, their gratuity; so that all talk of God has its foundation in the *esse* of creatures. This is not a reductionist view of God-talk (as though we were saying that all talk of God is 'really' about features of the world). It is not reductionist just because what is in question is their *esse* and this is not a feature of things that, for example, distinguishes them from other things: clearly we cannot set the class of existents over against a class of non-existents—not even an empty class of non-existents. We can however, as St Thomas points out, distinguish between nouns and noun-phrases such as 'the power of seeing' which refer to something that is, and terms such as 'blindness' which refer to an absence of what might have been expected to be. In that sense we can say that blindness is a non-being. We can also distinguish the sense in which a dog *is* and the irreducibly distinct sense in which his barking *is* or in which he *is* upside-down or *is* in Germany. We can distinguish, in fact, different categories of being. What we cannot do is set a class of existent things, activities or relations over-against a shadowy class of non-existent things, activities and relations. In a trivial sense you could say that what is common to absolutely everything is existence; but in saying this you would be conveying nothing at all: this Highest Common Factor is purchased at the cost of having no height at all. It is not in this way that *esse* is common to all—not, that is, as the asymptotic point at which specificity or determinateness vanishes altogether. No, *esse* is, in St Thomas' phrase, 'the actuality of every form', the determinately distinct actuality of every form.

For an Aristotelian, matter is what is relatively indeterminate and unstructured, waiting to be determined by some form or structure, the wood that may be made into the table, the table that may become part of the dining room suite. Matter in one form, one actualisation, is said to be potential with respect to being actualised by some other form. You never catch matter without some form or other. Form is the relatively determining factor giving being and intelligibility to a thing. With this in mind we can see that in a definition which is made by differentiating a genus (as the specific difference, rational, determines the genus, animal, in the classical definition of the human), the meaning of the genus word 'animal' is, in a sense, material, potential, open, waiting to be determined by the differentia word 'rational' which determines *in what sense* this is an animal. So to say that a human being is a rational animal is logically quite different from saying that a milkman is a man employed to deliver the milk; for men employed to deliver the milk and men not so employed are men in exactly the same sense; whereas rational and irrational animals are not animals in the same sense. Being rational is not an adventitious accidental feature of a general-purposes animal, it is having a certain (specific) kind of animality; whereas being employed to deliver the milk is an adventitious accidental feature of a general-purposes human being and does not signify a special kind of humanity. You never catch anything that is simply generically an animal without being differentiated as this or that species, just as you never catch matter which is not actualised and determined by some form. So, to repeat, genus words are 'open' (material) words that need to have their meaning 'closed' (formally) by a specific difference.

Now it is an Aristotelian thesis that *esse*, being, is not simply the widest, most all-embracing, most 'open' or material of genus words; it is not a genus at all. Cornelius Ernst puts it well:

> The community of the indefinite variety of all that is in *esse* is not only trans-generic in the sense that *ens* is found in all the genera (substance, quality, quantity and so on); it is trans-generic in the more fundamental sense that it is quite unlike the community of genus at all. For while the community of genus is subordinate and quasi-material, awaiting the formal determination of specific difference, the community of *esse* is superordinate and quasi-formal, the community of whatever has already achieved its appropriate differentiation as this or that discriminate individual: as [St Thomas] puts it in the *Summa Theologiae* (1a. 4, 1 ad 3): *ipsum esse est actualitas omnium rerum, et etiam ipsarum formarum* [*esse* is the actuality of all things including forms themselves]. Or again (1a. 8, 1) corp.): *Esse autem est illud quod est magis intimum cuilibet, et quod profundius omnibus inest, cum sit formale respectu omnium quae in*

re sunt [*esse* is that which is most intimate to each thing and what is in them most profoundly, for it is formative (*formale*) with respect to all that is in them.] (Thomas Aquinas 1964–81: vol XXX, Introduction, pp. xx–xxi).

To go back to the painter with his brush and his (and its) achievement: this achievement, that of being a work of art, is the ultimate actuality (cf. *esse*) which is the work of the painter in being the actuality of the paint-arranging (cf. trans-forming) achievement of the brush. The various works of Picasso may or may not have certain characteristic features in common, but when we say they are all Picasso's works we are not referring to these features or to any common feature, we are speaking simply of their common dependence on his action. The community of all things in *esse*, therefore, is their community as creatures of God, and it is this that is *das Mystische*.

The characteristic work of the paint-brush is to re-arrange paint, and simultaneously, in the same operation, the characteristic work of the artist wielding the brush is to make a painting: the work of the brush counts as painting because it is the work of the artist. It is thus the *esse* of things that leads us to speak of God—which for Wittgenstein in the *Tractatus* cannot be done. For him, we approach the mystical simply by recognizing the limits of what can be said. 'We feel that even if *all possible* scientific questions be answered, the problems of life have still not been touched at all. Of course there is then no question left, and just this is the answer.' (Wittgenstein 1933: 6.52)

St Thomas does not give up so easily. He sets himself to understand how language is used in the biblical tradition to which he belonged. He wholeheartedly agrees that we cannot say what God is, and he sets himself the task of understanding how we could speak of what, being the source of *esse* itself, is outside the scope of the world of existents, of what could not be an inhabitant of any world or subject to any of the intelligible limitations implied in being such an inhabitant, of what could not be one kind of thing rather than another, nor of course subject to the special limitations of material spatio-temporal beings, of what could not be *here* and *then*. We construct and learn the meanings of our language, and thus acquire our concepts, in coping with our world characterized by all these limitations, and intelligible precisely in terms of these limitations, in terms of forms which have their meanings as opposed to and distinct from other forms. No such concepts could possibly express what it means to be God.

Nevertheless, St Thomas concludes that there are two considerations which make it possible to give sense to the traditional biblical God-talk: first that we can understand what God is not, and second that we can use words not only to say what they mean but also to point beyond what we understand them to mean.

In listing just now the reasons for finding God unintelligible, I was pointing to just the negative knowledge which can form a basis not only for the negative statements I was making but for positive statements as well. Knowing what God is not can be a basis for saying (though not for understanding) what God is, or at least certain things about God. Let me give an example: God is intelligent (I think this may be what some people mean by saying that God is 'personal').

St Thomas regards both intelligence and intelligibility as a transcendence of material limitation. Sensation is necessarily subjective, rooted in this individual body with all its unique peculiarities. Because sensation is a kind of knowing, sensations are meanings. A meaning is always the role or function of some part in an organized structure—as, for instance, the meaning of a word is the part it plays in the language. The meaning which is a sensation is a bodily role, a meaning within the structure of my nervous system and brain. It is just in this way that sensing provides me with an interpretation of my world. Thus, for example, we determine whether a certain kind of animal has the sense of sight or not, not by looking to see if it has any eyes but by observing whether or not its behaviour (and hence its interpretation of the world) is any different when it is in the light or in the dark. It is because of this subjectivity of sensation that nobody else can have my sensation though, being the same kind of animal, they are likely to have similar ones. But with the advent of language we create a structure of meanings which is nobody's private domain. In principle nobody could have my sensation; but in principle everybody could have my thought. For the meanings of words are their roles not within the structure of any individual body but within the structure of language, which is in principle (in order to be language at all) shared by all. Because of the essential historicity of human language and human thought it may be impossibly difficult in practice to think the thoughts of Homer or Moses, but at least we would here be failing in a task; there is no such task as having the sensations of Homer or Moses or of the man next door. For St Thomas, what is bodily and material about me constitutes my privacy, my individuality; whereas my intellectual capacities liberate me from the prison of my subjectivity. My thought can never be just mine as my sensations are mine (there could scarcely be a greater contrast with the world of René Descartes). St Thomas did, however, think (and brilliantly argued in a little book called *De Unitate Intellectus*, which we may translate as *Is there only a single mind?*) that the act of *thinking* my thought is my own—because my capacity to think it is a capacity of my soul which is individuated as being the form of this individual material body: in this sense my thinking is mine just as my walking or digesting is mine. My thinking is *my* capacity to transcend my individuality; it is *my* thinking of meanings which are not just mine.

The point of that excursus was to make the connection between immateriality and understanding. For St Thomas' way of thinking, whatever is not subject to material limitation is intelligent. He thought rationality, our form of intelligence, was the lowest kind, being the activity of a being whose existence was as a material bodily being, though having a capacity to transcend purely bodily action. It is, however, the only kind of intelligence we are able partially to understand. Because intelligence belongs to the immaterial, if we deny materiality to God we must say he is intelligent. Because of a piece of negative knowledge, we can make this positive statement. But of course we are not saying that God has our kind of intelligence, that he is limited to rationality. We do not, in fact, understand the intelligence we are attributing to God. We can confidently assert that God is intelligent (or 'personal') while cheerfully admitting that we do not know what intelligence would be in God.

By similar processes of argument we can attribute to him goodness, justice, power and will without claiming to understand what these attributes would be in God. St Thomas, indeed, argues that having a multiplicity of attributes is itself a limitation that has to be denied of God. As they are in us, justice, mercy, intelligence and happiness are distinct characteristics: no such divisions could have place in God. God, indeed, could not *have* any characteristics as he does not *have* existence. The mystery of his intelligence and the mystery of his mercy and of his justice must be just the one mystery which is God. It cannot be one thing for him to exist and another for him to be wise and another for him to be good. The predicates we attach to the word 'God' have, indeed, different meanings in that their meaning is derived from our understanding of these things as properties in our world, but what they refer to in God is a single mystery which is quite unknown to us. We have some understanding of the wisdom that God creates in us, but when we say that God is wise we mean neither that he is the creator of wisdom in us, nor simply that he is not foolish; we mean that the quality we call wisdom in us exists in God in some higher and utterly mysterious way. (Cf. Thomas Aquinas 1964–81: vol. III, 1a. 13. 5)

If we are surprised that we should use the same words to refer in God to something quite different from what we use them to refer to in our world, St Thomas refers us to the common phenomenon of the analogous use of words. I may say that I love wine, my mistress, my country and my God, but nobody supposes that the word 'love' here signifies the same thing in each case. Nor does anyone suppose that I am merely making puns. It is common enough for a word to be used in different contexts with systematically different senses, with what St

Thomas would call a different *modus significandi*. St Thomas argues that this is just what happens with a great deal of our language about God, especially when we are doing theology: with, however, this special feature that in the case of God we do not (yet) understand the *modus significandi* of the words we use. That will have to wait for the beatific vision when we shall know God by sharing in his self-knowledge. St Thomas did also think that even in this life we may share, through faith, in that divine self-knowledge, but faith seems to us rather a darkness, an awareness of ignorance, than an intellectual clarity.

So for St Thomas, when we speak of God we do not know what we are talking about. We are simply taking language from the familiar context in which we understand it and using it to point beyond what we understand into the mystery that surrounds and sustains the world we do partially understand.

St Thomas, however, also insists that the greater part of our religious language is not, and should not be, understood in this way: most of the language we use in speaking of or to God is not even used analogically but metaphorically, by an appeal to images. What he calls *Sacra Doctrina*—meaning God's activity in teaching us in and through Scripture—requires, he says, such imaginative language. We need a great many images, preferably incompatible images (God is a mighty fortress, a still small voice, a vine-dresser, a mother eagle, he is wrathful and he is compassionate, he is faithful to his word but he repents of what he has done, and so on); moreover it is better to have many grotesque and base images (*sub figuris vilium corporum*), for all this preserves us from idolatry, from mistaking the image for God, from thinking of God as subject to the limitations of our imagery.

St Thomas distinguishes words like 'hearing', 'courageous', 'seeing', and 'wrathful', all of which have as part of their meaning a reference to what is material (you cannot be wrathful without the bodily emotions associated with aggression; you cannot see without eyes occupying a definite position in space) from words which, although we learn how to use them in bodily experience, do not have this physical reference as part of their meaning: as 'justice', for example, 'love' or 'goodness'. The former can only be used metaphorically, to provide images of the unknown God; the latter can be used to speak of him literally though only analogically, so leaving him still utterly mysterious to us.

For St Thomas, metaphor is the heart of religious language but it cannot be sufficient of itself. It needs to be underpinned by such non-metaphorical but analogical assertions as that God exists, that God is good, that God is the creative cause and sustainer of our world, that he is loving. It is these literal assertions that are subject to the caveat of analogy. Although we do not understand what they refer to in God, they are our way of asserting that the riches of religious imagery are more than the art-form of a particular culture (though, of course, they are that) but are part of our access to a mystery beyond our understanding which we do not create, but which rather creates us and our understanding and our whole world.

The Logic of Mysticism—II

CYRIL BARRETT

To talk of a *logic* of mysticism may sound distinctly odd. If anything, mysticism is alogical; it would be uncharitable if not false, on mature consideration, to call it illogical—though many, without due deliberation, might be tempted to use that term. Wittgenstein comes close to calling it illogical. In his lecture on ethics he draws attention to the logical oddity of statements of absolute value (Wittgenstein 1965). But he does not accuse the mystics or prophets or religious teachers of contradicting themselves or of invalid reasoning. What he accuses them of may be something worse, namely, talking nonsense, of not giving sense to the words they use or the expressions they utter. Russell (1921) and Ayer (1936) come to much the same conclusion but by a different route.

Fr McCabe has developed the Thomist account of religious language. As I find little with which to disagree in his account—though there are some things that I should like to emphasize and elaborate—I shall follow the line of the *Tractatus* which he eschewed. But first, and not solely for devilment, I shall examine the proposition that religious language in general and mystical writing in particular is illogical. In other words, I shall begin by seeming to be uncharitable. And I should consider that I had failed in my duty if I had left this aspect of religious language unexplored.

When Jesus says 'He that findeth his life shall lose it: and he that loseth his life for my sake shall find it' (Matthew x 39), he seems to be making contradictory statements. These statements are written off as paradoxes, modes of speech or tropes which *appear* to be contradictory but in fact are not, since the meanings of words change in midstream. This in itself is not logically very nice, but it will just about pass, since finding and losing life does not mean dying and being restored to *mortal* life. It is a close thing.

But what of Meister Eckhart's statement in his fourth German sermon that 'all creatures are pure nothing (*purum nihil*). I do not say that they are little or something; they are pure nothing' (Eckhart 1936: fascl. 24–45)? Surely here is a contradiction. A creature, to be a creature, must be something. A non-existent creature is no creature at all. But, then, we are told by Karrer, Copleston and others that this not what Eckhart means. In his case the trope is hyperbole or an exagger-

Cyril Barrett

ated use of language either for rhetorical emphasis or to express indirectly what cannot be directly expressed. In this case it is the low status of creaturely existence in comparison with divine existence. And for Eckhart God's existence is pretty dicy too. Sometimes Eckhart says that God is not a being; at others that nothing exists outside him, suggesting pantheism; and again that he is existence and that he is transcendent. Karrer (1926), De Wulf (1930) and Copleston (1953: III 183–95) among others have battled manfully to make sense out of all this and, though they disagree among themselves, have done a reasonably good job. But what it amounts to is to saying that Eckhart was trying to express the inexpressible. This led him to saying what, on the face of it, was absurd and nonsensical, verging on, if not over the edge of, the illogical.

Of the speculative mystics with whom we are dealing here, the one that went closest to the edge, if not over it, was Nicholas of Cusa. The work I have in mind is his famous *De docta ignorantia* (*On Learned Ignorance*; Nicholas of Cusa 1913). In this he writes of the *coincidentia oppositorum* ('the synthesis of opposites'). He believed, as did most mystics, that, in God, features that are as opposed as black is from white, good from evil, truth from falsehood, in some miraculous and mystical way come together and become reconciled genuinely—not in some fudged manner as black and white can become grey, or good and bad can become moderate behaviour, or truth and falsity are presented as possibilities or probabilities. Whether these would be the opposites reconciled in God or what the opposites are we are not told. What we are told is that in the case of any feature God is both the maximum and the minimum, the greatest and the least.

This is a real stinker. One can accept the proposition that God transcends degrees of goodness, knowledge and other qualities. And one can be content to accept that to do so is beyond our comprehension. But the notion that God not only transcends degrees but at the same time, in some mysterious way, *combines* the greatest and the least knocks comprehension into pulp. And this is precisely what Nicholas wants to do to us. This is the whole force of the title 'Instructed or Learned Ignorance'. He wants to hammer home the incomprehensibility of God. At the same time he wants to assert that this is in some way positive knowledge. It is not mere ignorance. It is learned ignorance, ignorance acquired after much thought. It is the arrival at the knowledge that God is, but is incomprehensible. Thus our ignorance of God is not common or garden ignorance but learned and instructed ignorance; that is, epistemic discretion: a refusal to claim knowledge and understanding that we cannot possess.

This, if I understand him correctly, is precisely Wittgenstein's position. In the *Tractatus* and the *Notebooks: 1914–1916* he writes of the mystical as inexpressible and pens the immortal line: '*Wovon man nicht sprechen kann, darüber muss man schweigen.*' (About that of which we cannot speak we must be silent; Wittgenstein 1933 & 1961(b): para. 7) He elaborates this in his lecture on ethics. There is no evidence that he was aware of Cusa's ideas, much less that he had read him (though one can never be sure about Wittgenstein's reading habits). Nevertheless, towards the end of the lecture he echoes Nicholas so closely that one might think he was giving a modern commentary on *De docta ignorantia*. Having shown to his own satisfaction and, indeed, to the satisfaction of most thinking people, that the notion of absolute values does not make sense, he then proposes a riposte that an absolutist might make. He might say: The reason why we have not been able to express absolute values is because we have not yet discovered the correct mode of expression. Wittgenstein rejects this suggestion with great vigour, and says that in rejecting it he sees clearly that the nature of ethical and religious expressions, expressions of absolute value, is that they are essentially nonsensical. They run against the limits of language and attempt to say the unsayable. (Wittgenstein 1965: 11–12) Yet, as he remarks in a conversation recorded by Waismann, 'the running up against something, *indicates something*' (Wittgenstein 1979: 69). He then quotes one of his favourite remarks from St Augustine's *Confessions* (I iv), '*et vae tacentibus de te, quoniam loquaces muti sunt*', which can be variously translated. Fairly literally it means: 'and woe to those who are silent about you [God], since the talkative are dumb'.[1] Wittgenstein's version ('*Was, du Mistviech, du willst keinen Unsinn reden? Rede nur einen Unsinn, es macht nichts!*') is rendered by Schulte and McGuinness as: 'What, you swine, you want not to talk nonsense! Go ahead and talk nonsense, it does not matter!' (Wittgenstein 1979: 69; cf Wittgenstein 1967: 69).

Fr McCabe is saying much the same sort of thing but invoking St Thomas Aquinas' arguments. Ironically, St Thomas' proofs for the existence of God were repulsive to Wittgenstein, as they were to Karl Barth whom Wittgenstein greatly admired.[2] Fr McCabe's effort is therefore a *tour de force*. Barth's and Wittgenstein's objection to *a posteriori* proofs for the existence of God was that (a) they make God part of the created universe—a prime mover, first in a chain of causes, that on which all depend, the highest in the degrees of being, the intelligence that orders the universe—robbing him of his transcenden-

---

[1] Translated in the Penguin edition by R. S. Pine-Coffin (Augustine 1961: 23): 'Yet woe betide those who are silent about you! For even those who are most gifted with speech cannot find words to describe you.'

[2] Particularly *Die kirchliche Dogmatik*. Barth is referred to (by name) at Wittgenstein 1980: 85.

tiality, and (b), and as a consequence, they make him to some extent intelligible and comprehensible.

Fr McCabe's ingenious answer to that is his play on the use of *esse* ('to be') by St Thomas. This is an odd word. It derives from Aristotle's τό εἶναι and is as odd in Greek as *esse*, as used by St Thomas, is in Latin or 'the to be' would be in English. And yet, paradoxically, it is its very oddness that makes it an appropriate instrument for expressing the mystical as Wittgenstein experienced it, that is as wonder that there is a world at all, not at how it came into being or how it shapes and reshapes itself, fascinating though all that is. As in so many other areas of philosophy St Thomas goes just that bit further than Wittgenstein. For St Thomas, as for St Anselm, only one being can exist essentially. In only one being *an est* and *quid est*, *esse* and *essentia* coincide. That is God. In the case of all other beings, otherwise known as creatures, *esse* or existence is coincidental: they could never have been and they may never be. This goes for the universe as a whole. Hence the wonder. Hence natural mysticism.

But does this quiet the distress of Barth and Wittgenstein? Does it prize God away from the world and establish his transcendence? He is still responsible for what exists in the universe and the existence of the universe itself. But he is neither in it nor does he *do* anything physically in it. As a mover, he does not shift gravel; as first cause does not have to keep our galaxy warm, encourage the fruit and veg. to grow, and keep the fauna relatively contented, nor organize the affairs and workings of the universe.

This may sound contrary to various scriptures where God is constantly interfering in human affairs and natural processes—working miracles (parting the Red Sea, stopping the sun, and so on), sending plagues, smiting the haughty, sending messages through his angels, bringing defeat to the infidel and so forth. It would be too glib and dishonest to say that this is a problem for theologians to solve. It is a problem for philosophers also, at least for those who believe both in the transcendence of God and also in divine providence. Some have an easier job than others. The Occasionalists, and also Leibniz and Berkeley, for instance, could say that God merely programmed the universe in some mysterious way and did not have to intervene. This answer presents almost as many problems as it solves, if it solves any. Space does not permit me to discuss them here, nor to offer a solution of my own.

The other objection Barth raised against the Thomist arguments concerns the use of analogy. According to Barth this is an attempt to put the transcendent God on a par with creatures in point of intelligibility, attributing to him human qualities albeit of a degree and order far beyond our comprehension. Nicholas of Cusa echoes this view (if an echo can be said to precede the sound it echoes) when he writes of learned ignorance about God, though, as we have seen, he reaches his goal by a different route.

Fr McCabe has given an able reply to this objection which I need not repeat. I endorse wholeheartedly what he says and in particular the following:

(1) The distinction between the metaphorical and imaginative use of language by religious writers in their desperate attempt—in Wittgenstein's phrases—'to express the inexpressible' and 'go beyond the boundaries of language', and theological language that attempts to make non-metaphorical assertions. Wittgenstein approved of the former. Indeed, he regarded them, as the only legitimate form of religious expression. The latter he regarded as a misguided way of saying, in some sort of scientific language, what cannot be said in scientific language. But, as Fr McCabe points out, the non-metaphorical expressions attempt to go beyond the capabilities of language just as much as metaphor and imagery do.

(2) The emphasis that St Thomas places on the unintelligibility of theological statements which is a logical consequence of the attempt to go beyond the bounds of language, 'beyond what we understand into the mystery that surrounds and sustains the world we do partially understand' (see above: 58).

(3) The treatment of analogy. Fr McCabe gives an account of analogy in terms of meaning and sense which is in line with modern thinking, particularly that of Wittgenstein. It is a great improvement on the usual Thomist and Scholastic account going back to John of St Thomas. The traditional account distinguishes between univocal, equivocal and analogical predication. In univocal predication the words used have the same meaning and sense, like 'energy' in different statements in physics or 'work' in mechanics for instance. In equivocal predication the words used have entirely different meanings, it is said. These are homonyms such as 'bank' and 'vice' which do not appear in other languages. No German would mistake an *Ufer* for a *Sparkasse* nor *das Laster* for *der Schraubstock*. (Puns are slightly different. They can play on sense as well as meaning. When the judge threatened to commit John Philpot Curran, he replied: 'That will not be the worst you have committed, my lord.') In analogical predication, it is said that words are used with partly the same meaning and partly a different one.[3]

This, as it stands, is hardly comprehensible. How can the meaning of a word be divided into one part that can be the same as a part of another

[3] Later Scholastics were to describe analogy as *aequivocato e concilio*, thus placing emphasis on the equivocal element.

meaning and a part that can be different? Attempts have been made to achieve this feat. As might be expected, these attempts were made with the aid of formal logic (cf Bochenski 1948 and Ross 1961). The trick is to find a factor that is common to both or all those things, properties, relations, etc. to which the words are applied. This part of the meaning is deemed to be univocal. The part that is different is deemed to be equivocal. Thus an analogical meaning is a hybrid, partly univocal, partly equivocal. This kind of conceptual surgery can just about pass in the *classification* of Nature. Humans have in common with mice and geraniums that they are organisms. Humans and mice differ from geraniums in that they are sentient. But no such separation as this exists *in* Nature. Humans do not have a rational part, a sentient part and a vegetative part that can be separated off, except in the mind. Further, the idea of splitting meaning into a part that is the same and a part that is different makes no sense at all. If the meaning of words is different in any respect, the *words are different*, and hence the use of them together would be equivocal.

The whole point of analogical predication is that the meaning remains the same (univocal) but the *sense* is different. That is to say, the use to which the word is put may vary but the meaning remains the same. To illustrate this from examples closer to our subject, take the word 'good'. There are those who say it has a different meaning when used of a boeuf stroganoff, a spin-dryer, a work of art, a tennis player, a neighbour, a religious man and God. If the meanings of the words are different, the question then arises why we describe them all by the same word 'good'. We could say the beef was very tasty, the dryer very efficient, the work of art outstandingly competent and aesthetically pleasing, the tennis player more than competent at the game, and so on. And yet—*and yet*—we choose, without any seeming semantic impropriety, to use the word 'good' of all of them. Is it being suggested that the word 'good' as said of food is a synonym for 'tasty' and of a spin-dryer for 'efficient'? If this were so, it would make 'good' an equivocal term, like 'bank' and 'vice'. Thus, there should be 'tasty good' and 'efficient good' as distinct from each other in meaning as 'river bank' from 'savings bank'. In that case, we could substitute other words for tasting good and good performance. Let us call them 'tas' and 'fic'. And let us compare them with *Ufer* and *Sparkasse*.

To explain what an *Ufer* is one does not have to say anything about savings banks or commercial lending houses or investment institutions. One talks about rivers, streams and canals. But to say why a tasty meal is good one has to say something about what it is for anything to be good, why we use this word of diverse things. It must have a meaning that traverses all its uses. In the case of 'good' we have just such a meaning. In each case 'good' is an expression of approval: a good dish is one we approve of, a good machine is one we approve of, and so on. That is sufficient to explain why we use the same homonym in each case. There is no need for 'tas' and 'fic'. They would serve no useful purpose, except perhaps to distinguish what is gastronomically *good* from what is utilitarianly *good*; but that is superfluous. What differs in each case is not the meaning but the *sense* or use to which we put a word. This will vary with the object to which the word is applied, the context of application, etc.

To return to talk about God. There is no need to say that words used of him have an *entirely different* meaning, as Barth seems to imply, or even that they have a *partially different* meaning from words used of creatures, as some Scholastics would have us believe. They have a different sense certainly. God is not good to eat or useful and efficient or proficient, nor even good as a citizen, neighbour or holy person is good. Unlike good things and persons, we do not know in what the goodness of God consists. All we know is that he is something to be approved of and is, in some way, the source of every kind of goodness. As Wittgenstein says, in using terms such as 'good', 'powerful', 'intelligent', 'just', 'merciful', etc. of God we are pushing out beyond the boundaries of language into the unknown. But we are doing so by means of language and of what is known. And we are doing so in order to understand the known better.

Here it might be helpful to consider the analogy of the discovery of the planet Neptune in 1845 by the mathematician J.C. Adams in England and, independently, in 1846 by Leverrier in France. In 1781 Sir William Herschel, by means of a telescope, discovered the seventh planet, named Uranus, which is barely visible to the naked eye and has not been revealed in detail until recently. Its orbit showed perturbations that could not be accounted for by the position and orbits of the other known six planets or the sun. Adams and Leverrier calculated that there must be another, hitherto unknown, planet in orbit (mean distance 2793 million miles) around the sun. In 1846 the astronomer Galle found it by means of a telescope, but again with little detail. So it is possible to probe into the unknown from the known where the known is problematical.

Of course the analogy breaks down, as do they all. The main point of breakage is that, whereas what Adams and Leverrier were doing was calculation, what the mystics and theologians are doing most definitely is not, whatever it is. Moreover, the scientists had a definite concept of the sort of thing they were looking for and one of its qualities, i.e. gravitational attraction, whereas the mystics and theologians do not have such concepts. Nevertheless, when they started their calculations the scientists did not *know* what they might find or what form that force might take. That it was a *planet* was discovered by Galle. The force of

Cyril Barrett

the analogy is to show that to press from the known into the unknown via the problematical is not the preserve of mystics and theologians. It is a natural tendency in all human beings that are intellectually aware. Of course, the intellectual courage that drove Kepler and Galileo and, to a lesser extent, Adams and Leverrier to plunge into the unknown is quite different from that of the mystics and mystical theologians. The former were going from the known to the, presumably, not dissimilar, or at least recognizable in familiar terms. The mystics plunge from the known into the deep unknown. The first find aspects of science problematical and venture forth cutting new paths of knowledge and understanding. The second not only find science problematical but find that, in Wittgenstein's words, 'even if *all possible* scientific questions be answered, the problems of life have still not been touched at all' (Wittgenstein 1933: 6.52).

'The problems of life', the question 'not *how* the world is . . . but *that* it is' (6.44) and many such problems, are not scientific problems. They cannot be answered by any kind of calculation or logical reasoning. Why then—to return to my original remarks—talk of the logic of mysticism? That I take to be a shock title designed to emphasize the contrast between mysticism and logic. It might have been less provocatively phrased as 'the logical status of mysticism'. It makes complete sense to speak of the logical status of mysticism, just as it does to speak of the logical status of fiction or fairytales or poetry or literary and art criticism. This does not mean that they are in themselves logical, i.e. follow strict rules of logic, which they clearly do not, but rather that they have their place in—to quote a Wittgenstein phrase and put it to another use—'logical space'. That is to say, we can ask (a) whether they are logical in the strict sense; (b) whether, if they are not, they have any meaning; (c) if they have, what it is, how is it to be described and characterized; (d) how is it to be related to expressions that are regarded as logical. For instance, one can ask about fiction whether it has meaning since it has no referents. No Noble Knight of La Mancha, no Falstaff, no Mr Pickwick or Mr Macawber ever existed. With fairytales and the like it is worse. There never were any leprechauns, or hares, rabbits and other beasts that talk. And as for poetry, it is unverifiable. How do we know, to quote Yeats, that 'the wind that awakened the stars /Is blowing through my blood'?

To show that these are irrelevant questions, that they totally miss the point is, in itself, a logical activity. So is it to indicate the use of words in religious and mystical discourse. And here I should like to issue a caveat. It is tempting to think of mystics as a special breed of religious believers. They are not. If Wittgenstein is correct, anyone who has a religious experience is a mystic and even those who have no religious beliefs can have mystical experiences. It is only that the professional mystics, such as Eckhart and Nicholas of Cusa, sound more outrageous than the rest; but genuinely to believe in the Incarnation and Redemption is no less mystical. It flies in the face of commonsense and logic. Logic puts it in its place. Its place is *not to be logical*, but not to be illogical either.

It is fundamental to any philosophy of religion to realize that it must be firmly based on a logic of religious language, and that religious language is itself mystical, that is, an attempt to express the inexpressible. To overlook this is to make giant strides in the wrong direction, as many philosophers have done. These include some who regard themselves as religious as well as those antagonistic to religion. They treat philosophy of religion as a branch of natural philosophy. The former believe that they can provide positive knowledge about the nature of God.[4] The latter, realizing that this is impossible, dismiss religion as empty, meaningless and superstitious.[5]

It may be harsh to say that in talking about God we do not know what we are talking about (or not much), that we are trying to express the inexpressible and are banging our heads against the boundaries of what can be said. But is that not preferable to thinking we know what we are talking about when we do not?

[4] Apologists such as Fr J. O'Hara (1931: 107–116).
[5] Positivists such as Comte, Taine, the Vienna Circle, Ramsey, Ayer and, more recently, Kai Neilsen.

The Meaning of 'God'—I

MICHAEL DURRANT

Introduction

In this paper I shall be examining the following claims:

(1) that 'God' has no meaning, in the sense of 'sense'; that it is a proper name analogous to a Russellian proper name in that it has reference only. More crudely, that we cannot describe God in any way but only name Him and refer to Him by name;[1]

(2) that 'God' has no meaning, in the sense of 'sense' in that the nature of God is fundamentally inexpressible. That God is, as some have said, 'wholly other' or even 'the wholly other'.

Having contended that neither (1) nor (2) are plausible, I shall then raise the question of what it is to offer an account of the meaning of a word. For present purposes I put forward a Wittgensteinian account in terms of 'use' mentioning various uses of the term 'God' in Christian activity. I then ask whether the uses mentioned rest upon a more basic use or meaning. I shall hold that they do so rest upon a more basic use or meaning—a 'descriptive' use or meaning.

I then turn to the problem that 'God' in Christian Theology appears to have no single descriptive use or meaning but rather a variety of such uses or meanings some of which seem incompatible with one another in more or less radical ways. I shall consider four approaches to this problem highlighting it by reference to what Thomas Morris (1987b) specified as a 'great divide' in the 'creative chaos of contemporary thought about God'.

Finally, I offer some concluding thoughts as to the path forward though I do not claim that this is a new path. It is an old well worn one.

---

[1] I am not here implicitly introducing the thesis that proper names are 'rigid designators'. The 'rigid designator' thesis, as I understand it, does not necessarily deny that proper names have a sense but holds that they have no definite sense in any actual system of discourse representing any actual world. *Aristotle*, for example, will only possess in all possible worlds such properties as are essential to his being Aristotle. On other grounds I should wish to reject the 'rigid designator' theory of names and the 'causal' theory of reference but this is not the place to pursue the matter. I present some implicit criticisms in my discussion of Soskice (see also Durrant 1989).

Michael Durrant

I

(1) To consider the thesis that 'God' has no meaning, in the sense of 'sense', but reference only, analogous to a Russellian proper name. This thesis assumes that 'God', in its use in Christian Theology, is construed at least as a proper name. Professor Geach long ago argued that this is not the case and I myself have similarly argued. (Anscombe and Geach 1961: 'Aquinas'; Durrant 1973b) 'God' admits of the plural form and the indefinite article and can be prefaced by 'many', 'several', 'one', which no proper name ever does, as Frege (1950: paras 50–53) rightly observed. Further, it is only if 'God' is construed as an 'affirmatively predicable' term (Anscombe and Geach 1961: 89) that it is possible to affirm that God exists, that there is a god.[2]

Further, to hold that 'God', even if a proper name, has no sense but reference only gives rise to the following objection. If 'God' has no sense, if we are unable to give any description of Him which would convey the sense, then (a) how would we determine that if you say 'God divided the Red Sea into two parts and let the Israelites go through' and I say 'God divided the Red Sea . . .' we are both referring to one and the same thing, entity? Both you and I may only speak of referring to the *same* thing in our respective uses of the proper name 'God' if we are able in some sense to say *what it is* that we are putatively referring to. If we can offer *no* account of the sameness of what we are putatively referring to, then we cannot speak of referring to the same thing for there is no such X as 'sameness' which is not sameness in relation to something or other. If I assert that John and Peter are the same, this calls forth the question: 'the same *what*?'—'the same man'; 'the same cat'. As Geach has argued: 'For every proper name there is a corresponding use of a common noun preceded by "the same", to express what requirements as to identity the proper name conveys . . .'; and again: '. . . it makes no sense to judge whether *x* and *y* are "the same", or whether *x* remains "the same", unless we add or understand some general term—"the same F"' (Geach 1962: 43–44; 39). Thus we may only speak of you and me referring to the same individual by the alleged proper name 'God' if we are able to say that we are both referring to the same F, where 'F' supplies a criterion of identity for the name. This entails that what is putatively referred to by the proper name 'God' must, in crude terms, be describable. To claim that 'God' or indeed any proper name has reference only forbids its use *as* a proper name, for part of the function of an ordinary proper name is our ability to use it on more than one occasion to refer to *the same* individual.[3]

[2] It is clear from Professor Geach's reply to this paper that we are agreed that 'God' is grammatically a common noun.

[3] Here, on points of substance, Geach and I are in agreement.

Dr Janet Martin Soskice in her recent book *Metaphor and Religious Language* claims that we may only *name* God and never describe Him; that 'God' is, in effect, a proper name that has reference only. She claims that as concerns God we may only 'point towards Him' and not describe Him. It is on the ground that we may not describe God that she rejects the application to her own 'critical realism' of the customary criticism of the 'realist' in theology, for the realist (as opposed to the 'critical realist') claims to describe God (Soskice 1985: 140). However if one may not describe God in any way as Soskice demands, but only 'point towards Him' by the use of the proper name 'God', then how may one (a) intelligibly claim that one is pointing towards *Him*?—to so intelligibly claim God must already be thought to be a person or analogous to a person; (b) claim that one is 'pointing towards'? I may only claim that I am pointing towards something in my use of an expression if I can at least offer *some* description of what it is I am pointing towards—otherwise how can I ever claim that I have been or currently am *successful* in my pointing? And if I cannot say what would constitute success or failure in my pointing towards then how can I speak of 'pointing towards' at all?

The thesis that we may not at all describe God but only point towards Him breaks down at this point. Indeed in a recent paper (Durrant 1989) I have argued that Soskice's account of and her defence of a 'critical realist' position in theology breaks down in many other ways, e.g., that her general theory of reference is deficient, but I shall not pursue these technicalities here. Traditional Christian Theology in the Catholic tradition, as I understand it, does not commit us (a) to the thesis that 'God' is a proper name and hence a proper name that has reference only; (b) to the view that 'God' has no meaning in the sense of 'sense'; (c) to the view that God cannot in any sense be described. St Thomas Aquinas, for example, denies that 'God' is a proper name (and hence a proper name that has reference only) and whilst holding that we cannot know what God is—we can only know what He is not—it does not follow from this that we cannot describe God in any way. God is said to be simple, perfect, limitless, unchangeable and one (Thomas Aquinas 1964–81: vol. II, 1a. 3). He is further said to be good by nature (Ia. 6, 3) and supremely good (Ia. 6, 2). This gives us at least part of the sense of 'God'; any F (nature) which did not exhibit at least these characteristics would not be God.[4, *]

---

[4] Geach and I are in agreement concerning the restricted range of answers to the Aristotelian '$\tau\acute{\iota}\ \acute{\varepsilon}\sigma\tau\iota\nu$;' question—St Thomas' '*quid sit?*' question—and we do not take it for granted that 'this medieval stuff' has long since been shown worthless by the labours of John Locke. I further concur with Geach that 'if someone should compare our present knowledge of God to Lockyer's knowledge of helium, he

(2) I now turn to the thesis that 'God' has no meaning in the sense of 'sense' in that the nature of God is fundamentally inexpressible. That God is, as some have said, 'wholly other' or even '*the* wholly other'. In that it is held that what God is is fundamentally and absolutely inexpressible then the position is paradoxical, for on this account in saying that God's nature is fundamentally inexpressible we have already described God's nature—namely that it is fundamentally inexpressible. In other words those who advocate this position cannot do so without contradicting themselves. It will however be protested that this paradox is necessarily avoidable. An advocate will point out that to say that God's nature is fundamentally inexpressible is not to give a description of God's nature but to give a remark of 'logical grammar'; it is not to describe God's nature but precisely to say that it is not describable. Even so I contend the thesis is in radical difficulty. If God's nature *is* so fundamentally indescribable, inexpressible, then we can never in principle refer to God or claim of *Him* that *He* did certain marvellous acts. We could never on such a thesis say, for example, 'God divided the Red Sea into two parts' or 'God raised Jesus from the dead'. What precisely is involved in the claim that God is 'wholly other' is unclear. If it is the claim that God, in principle, is unable to be described in human terms then we are once again in a paradox for we have to use human terms to say *that*. Further, if it is construed as the claim that God is unable to be categorized in human thought—that God is *whatever it is* that is unable to be categorized in human thought—then we have the problem that the very use of 'whatever it is' implies categorisation, for one has spoken of 'whatever it is'. As for the claim that God is *the* wholly other, I surmise that this is the claim that God is that single thing which is unable to be categorized in human thought. Once again, however, categorisation is implicit for one has spoken of 'that single thing', that single F.

II

Having rejected (1) and (2) and taking these as exhaustive, I am committed to the thesis that 'God' has meaning, has a 'sense', and so I now turn to the question of the meaning (or meanings) of 'God'. First, however, I must raise the question of what it is for a word to have sense

---

would not be saying something obviously absurd, nor yet refuting himself in every affirmation he made about God'. I may consistently so concur for I am holding that we may affirm something truly of God, that we may truly describe God, even though we may not know concerning God *quid sit*.

* See additional note at the conclusion of this paper (page 84).

or meaning. For present purposes I shall adopt a suggestion of Wittgenstein[5] namely, that an account of the meaning of a word is to be
given in terms of its use in practice; its use in a 'language-game'. *Ergo*
the meaning of the word 'God' is its use in practice, in the 'language-
game', 'form of life' of the Christian believer or more generally, in the
'language-game', 'form of life' of the Christian religion. In one clear
sense however 'God' has many different uses within this 'form of life'.
We may use 'God' as part of a sentence in which we give praise to Him as
in Psalm cl: 'O praise God in his holiness; praise him in the firmament
of his power'; or again to petition Him to have mercy upon us as in the
great penitential Psalm li: 'Have mercy upon me, O God, after thy great
goodness . . .'; or again to petition Him to make us aright with Him:
'Turn thy face from my sins, and put out all my misdeeds. Make me a
clean heart O God; and renew a right spirit within me' (li 9–10); or
again, to magnify Him and rejoice in Him—as in the *Magnificat*. We
cannot hold however that in all these different uses of 'God', we have
different *meanings*. Intuitively one certainly wants to hold that the
term 'God' has the same meaning in all these various uses and that these
uses rest upon a more basic use or meaning. One wants to hold that
'God' has the *same* meaning in all these uses in that the same F is
praised, petitioned, magnified, etc., and that these uses rest upon a
more basic meaning or use in that, for example, one praises God for
what He is and what He has done and continues to do; one petitions
God for what He is able to do. This more basic meaning or use I shall
designate as the *descriptive* meaning or use.

III

I am now faced with a central problem. I have claimed that an appeal to
what I have designated 'descriptive' meaning or use has to be made for
other uses of 'God' to be intelligible. Yet within Christian Theology
and tradition, and certainly within Christian philosophising, there
appears to be no single descriptive meaning or use for the term 'God'.
Thomas Morris draws our attention to this both in his 'Introduction' to
his recent collection *The Concept of God* and most particularly in his
paper 'The God of Abraham, Isaac and Anselm' in his collection
Anselmian Explorations. There are, for example, 'those who conceive
of God as impassible, immutable, atemporal and metaphysically simple', and those who think of God 'as a ceaselessly changing, perfectly
responsive temporal agent continually interacting with created, temporal beings' (Morris 1987a: 6). More specifically he writes:

[5] Wittgenstein 1958: 69; 1953: I, para. 43. See also: 'You might say . . . of a
word, "Its meaning is its purpose".' (Wittgenstein 1975: 59)

Michael Durrant

Within the creative chaos of contemporary thought about God, there is at least one great divide. On one side are those who work in the *a priorist*, Anselmian tradition which begins with a purportedly self-evident conception of God as the greatest possible being. . . . On the other side of the divide are those who are committed to an *a posteriori*, empirical, or experiential mode of developing our idea of God. These theologians most commonly take as their starting point and touchstone for truth the data of religious experience and biblical revelation.

And later we have:

Those who draw their sustenance from the pages of scripture and the day to day realities of religious experience are for their part apt to contrast starkly the God of faith with the God of reason, the God of history with the God of the academy, the God of Abraham, Isaac and Jacob with the God of the philosophers . . . (Morris 1987b: 10)

Faced with this 'great divide'[6] and with at least two different and seemingly incompatible descriptive meanings or uses for 'God', how are we to resolve the difficulty? I shall consider four approaches.

A. The first approach would be to deny that one of the descriptive meanings represented true Christian thinking about God. To adopt this approach, whichever descriptive meaning was advocated, would be to deny a whole tradition of Christian thought and a whole approach to Theology.[7] For those who might hold that the God of 'reason' has no

---

[6] Geach finds the presentation of the alleged difference between the God of Philosophy and the God of the Christian believer puzzling, and even more importantly he finds it very odd when an Anselmian God is *contrasted* with the God of the Christian believer. I think it fair to point out that I do not actually use the term 'Christian believer'. The contrast introduced is that introduced by Morris and I am not claiming that 'those who think of God as a ceaselessly changing, perfectly responsive temporal agent continually interacting with created temporal beings' are the true Christian believers. I apologise if I have given this impression. Further, I am not holding that an 'Anselmian' God *is* to be contrasted with the God of the Christian believer; I am simply reflecting a contrast which has been drawn. As Morris expresses the matter: 'Those who draw their sustenance from the pages of scripture and the day to day realities of religious experience are for their part apt to contrast starkly the God of faith with the God of reason . . .'. Geach presents an argument for saying that no such contrast exists for *St Anselm*, but from the fact that no such contrast exists for St Anselm it does not follow that no such contrast has been drawn. Geach would hold, I surmise, that to draw such a contrast is *misguided*. In fairness to him I cannot pursue this matter further here; I must simply note the point.

[7] In fact it is not always possible to draw such a clear cut divide but that there is a divide seems *prima facie* clear.

part to play in religious belief, one could, for example, refer them to the first of the Thirty-Nine Articles of the Church of England which reads: 'There is but one living and true God, everlasting, without body, parts, or passions; of infinite power, wisdom, and goodness . . .' For those who might hold that the object of religious devotion is impassible, immutable, atemporal, then what of the belief that God is continually interacting with his creatures and is indeed responsive to their prayers?

B. A second approach would be to hold that although we seem to be faced with at least two different and apparently incompatible descriptive meanings or uses, there is ultimately no fundamental divide since these meanings may be held to converge. That indeed, as Morris (1987b) has recently argued, this deep divide in theology, or perhaps meta-theology, can and should be bridged. He claims that an interesting *prima facie* case can be made for holding that the God of St Anselm *is* the God of the Patriarchs. In spite of its sophistication and considerable interest I shall claim that his case is not conclusive.

To get down to the particular details of Morris' thesis. He wants to argue that under two simple conditions the very different ways of thinking about God can be rationally held to converge. He hopes to show that if the object of worship in the Judaeo-Christian tradition is indeed intended to be God—the ultimate reality responsible for the existence and activity of everything else—and if the Anselmian conception (of God) is coherent, then it can be quite reasonable to hold that the God of St Anselm *is* one and the same as the God of Abraham, Isaac and Jacob, the God and Father of Jesus the Christ.

I shall not here be concerned with the question of whether the Anselmian conception *is* coherent and hence with Morris' attempts to defend its coherence against attack. *My* question is: '*Granted* the Anselmian conception *is* coherent, does Morris conclusively make out a *prima facie* case for holding that the God of St Anselm is one and the same (god) as the God of the Patriarchs and of Our Lord Jesus Christ?

He sets forth a simple yet forceful thought experiment which has the appearance of showing that the Anselmian description of God does not capture the 'properly religious' conception at all. The thought experiment is as follows:[8]

[8] Geach finds himself unable to make the 'thought experiment' outlined by Morris. The parity he makes between the mathematical example and Morris' thought experiment, I understand, is simply the parity of absurdity. In the light of private correspondence I would now concur with Geach's bafflement concerning the idea of *discovering* or *finding out* that a being knowledgeable but not omniscient, etc., is in point of fact someone who created and sustains the world, for, as Geach has pointed out to me, the question arises: 'Finding out *how*?'—'By some empirical observation?' or 'Because the being himself revealed it?' If the latter the problem clearly arises that such a being might be

Michael Durrant

> Suppose we somehow discovered a less than Anselmian being, an individual who was very powerful but not strictly omnipotent, very knowledgeable but not literally omniscient, and very dependable but not altogether immutable, etc., had created our universe and was responsible for the existence of intelligent life on earth. Suppose we found that he had been the one to call Abraham out of Ur, to speak to Moses, and to send the prophets. Suppose he had somehow become incarnate in the man Jesus, and that he will be the one responsible for giving eternal bliss to all who are properly related to him. Let him even sustain directly the very existence of the universe moment to moment. Would we rightly on *a priori* grounds refuse to call him "God", just because he did not satisfy St Anselm's precise requirements?' (Morris 1987b: 19)

Morris concedes that the common reply would be: 'of course not'; if he is the being the Bible is about, then Jews and Christians would just be committed to acknowledging him as God. And he adds (19–20): 'Few if any people would doubt whether the Anselmian formula specifies a sufficient condition for deity. But many would deny that it presents a necessary one. And this is what our brief thought experiment could be taken to show. . . . Our thought experiment can appear to show that St Anselm's concept of God just is not the Judeo-Christian concept.'

Our author however is out to show that it *is*, so how does he seek to show that such a being as above characterized would *not* be the God of Judaeo-Christian thought? He first draws our attention to an important feature of the Anselmian conception. Such a conception entails that among the properties of a maximally perfect being is that of being necessarily existent or existent in every possible world. Hence if the Anselmian conception as a whole is coherent, or more exactly if maximal perfection is possibly exemplified, then it is necessarily exemplified as well. Having made this point Morris returns to the thought experiment. The less than perfect being of the experiment, less than Anselmian being, is designated 'El' and the world in which he accomplishes his prodigious feats, *W*. We then have the following argument:

> If Anselmianism is coherent, the theist who follows Anselm in his way of thinking about God can plausibly hold that an Anselmian

---

mistaken. To this one might conjecture that Morris would reply that one can imagine that a knowledgeable but less than omniscient being created and sustains the world; the *idea* of a less than omniscient being, i.e. a limited being, creating and sustaining the world is not an impossible one. To this I think it would be fair to say that Geach would reply that no being other than an omniscient one *could* be the creator and sustainer of the world, for if X is less than omniscient then X itself is a created being. Clearly however the matter cannot be further pursued here and it remains an open question as to whether Morris would so reply.

being exists in some possible world. But by virtue of being necessary, he exists in every other world as well, including W. Now if in W there is a being who is omnipotent, omniscient, and all the rest, surely El is *not* God, but rather, at best, the vicegerent or deputy of God, a sort of demiurge. If El is less than omnipotent, and there is an omnipotent, omniscient individual, then clearly anything El accomplishes is done only at the good pleasure . . . of the Anselmian being. El would not be the ultimate reality. He would not be God. I think this conclusion is fully in accord with the properly religious usage of 'God' in Judeo-Christian orthodoxy, and in fact that it is a conclusion forced on us by that usage. If the object of worship in the western tradition of theology is intended to be the ultimate reality, and if the Anselmian conception of God is coherent . . . then the God of religious devotion is the God of the philosophers. (Morris 1987b: 20)

Does the argument work? Central to answering in the affirmative is Morris' first condition, namely, that the object of worship in the Judaeo-Christian tradition is intended to be God in the sense of the ultimate reality responsible for the existence and activity of everything else. This condition whilst necessarily vague surely cannot be denied.

Morris' strategy is then to argue that any being (say El) exhibiting features less than those exhibited by an Anselmian God would not be such an ultimate reality and hence would not be God. This supposes that *only* an x which exhibits the features an Anselmian God exhibits *could* be the ultimate reality responsible for the existence of everything else, and Morris does not conclusively show that this is the case. He convincingly shows that El could not be God; that any being exhibiting those features is less than God, but he does not show (a) that a being exhibiting the features of being 'a ceaselessly changing, perfectly responsive temporal agent continually interacting with created, temporal beings' is identical with El; nor (b) that any being exhibiting the features of an Anselmian God is identical with the ultimate reality responsible for the existence of everything else. Any such ultimate reality, we might argue, must exhibit at least the features which an Anselmian God exhibits, but why at the *most* those features? It is only if Morris can show that ultimate reality must exhibit at the most those features that an Anselmian God can be said to exhibit, that an Anselmian God can be said to be identical with the ultimate reality and hence that the God of religious devotion (in his parlance) can be said to be the God of the philosophers. Morris assumes that a being exhibiting Anselmian features is *sufficient* for deity; he has written: 'Few if any people would doubt whether the Anselmian formula specifies a sufficient condition for deity', but I hold that he does not show this. He is concerned to argue that it is after all a necessary condition and, having argued this and assumed it is a sufficient condition, he then contends that the God of St Anselm is identical with the ultimate reality and since the God of the Patriarchs and of Jesus is identical with the ultimate reality, the God of St Anselm is identical with the God of the Patriarchs and Jesus.

This neat and sophisticated attempt to 'bridge the gap', I have argued, fails. Indeed for it to succeed would further require that the concept of 'God' as the greatest possible or maximally perfect being, as exemplifying necessarily a maximally perfect set of compossible great-making properties, is one which (a) any rational person and (b) any Christian as a rational person has to accept. Now I do not think it can be denied that the Christian believer accepts, acknowledges, God to be the greatest possible, maximally perfect, being and X could not be a maximally perfect being if X did not exemplify necessarily a maximally perfect set of compossible great-making properties. The problem is that the set of great-making properties (i.e. those which it is intrinsically better for a being to have than to lack) for the Christian God would appear to contain not only those attributed by St Anselm (or Anselmians)—e.g., being omnipotent, immutable, omniscient, eternal—but *also* being personal, merciful, loving, forgiving, concerned with the welfare of human beings and other forms of life on this earth. My concern, as I have indicated earlier, is not with any alleged incompatibility which may arise between the great-making properties which St Anselm (or Anselmians) ascribe to God (e.g., the alleged incompatibility between being omnipotent and being perfect) but with the seeming incompatibility between such properties and *other* great-making properties which Christian theology and tradition have ascribed to God.

C. A third approach would be to agree that 'God' has not a single descriptive meaning; that the concept of 'God' presents us with at least two differing but related meanings. Christian thought is not guilty of equivocation and hence the problem arises as to how the differing meanings are related—what forms the unifying principle for these apparently differing meanings? Clearly what forms the unifying principle cannot be a further descriptive meaning or sense; such a principle must be of a higher order. Here one may make the suggestion that what unifies these apparently different senses is a common function, namely, they both have the function of describing an object, in the broadest sense—a nature—of worship worthiness. To say that God is an object worthy of worship is not to describe God; it is not to give a further descriptive meaning or sense but rather, as Morris argues, to allocate a higher order role to 'God' or to give ontological status to God. He writes:

For instance a good many philosophers nowadays think of deity or divinity as a role, or office, or ontological status which a particular individual will have, or fail to have, depending upon what other properties that individual has. On this way of thinking, deity is something like a second-order attribute, much like the attribute of worship-worthiness. An individual who has the second-order property of worship-worthiness will have it in virtue of having other, first-order properties, such as the property of being good, or the property of being holy. More precisely, from this point of view as standardly explicated, deity will be a higher-order property, perhaps a third-or-more-order property, in virtue of depending upon or containing second-order properties such as worship-worthiness, as well as first-order properties such as goodness. In any case, deity or divinity—the property of being God—is commonly understood along these lines in such a way as to support conceptual truths about God, propositions which are necessarily true, and can in some sense be known *a priori*. (Morris 1987a: 4)

The problems with this approach are:

(i) it is an entirely *a priori* approach which will be objected to by those who do not subscribe to such an approach in theology;

(ii) even within such an approach, as Morris acknowledges: 'the question of whether a particular array of attributes can be constitutive of deity, or can be thought in any way to characterize God, will turn in part on a consideration of whether precise analyses of those attributes show them to be compossible or mutually consistent.' (5) Within the context of an *a priorist* approach, say we were to hold on *a priori* grounds that it is a necessary truth that whatever is an object of worship-worthiness also exhibit the features of being personal and showing care for the welfare of the worshippers, we are still faced with the question of whether the properties 'being personal' and 'showing concern for our welfare' are compatible with the properties standardly attributed to the God of St Anselm.

D. A fourth approach would be to adopt that advocated by Charles Hartshorne in his well known but by now rather old paper 'The God of Religion and the God of Philosophy'. What Hartshorne holds is that:

The standard terms of religious philosophising—absolute, infinite, immutable, eternal, self-sufficient, necessary, universal cause—do apply to the God of religion, but they apply less simply and exclusively than has been supposed. God is *somehow* absolute, infinite, immutable, and supreme cause; but in such fashion that he can *also* be relative, finite, mutable, and supreme effect. God comes under both sides of the basic contraries. On both sides he is different in principle from other individuals. He is cause in a radically unique or 'eminent' sense; he is also effect in an equally unique sense; he is infinite as no one else is, but also finite as no one else is. I call this the 'principle of dual transcendence'. (Hartshorne 1969: 162–3)

He adds that he could and indeed has filled volumes on this topic but that all he has space to do in this paper is give 'a few glimpses of the relevant system of ideas'.

I trust I am not being unfair to Hartshorne in tackling here just his basic account; I have not the time or space for more.

First, I would observe (a) that I know of no part of the admittedly complex Christian tradition which actually regards God as an effect or as finite in whatever unique or special sense. More importantly, (b) Hartshorne claims that God is cause in a radically unique or 'eminent' sense and that he is effect in an equally unique sense. The problem arises as to *what* sense. There can be *no* 'radically unique' sense of 'cause' which applies and which *can* apply *only* to a single individual however eminent, for this would turn 'cause' from being a general term, which in principle has application to more than one thing (though in fact may only apply to one thing), into a sort of proper name, which cannot be said to have application *at all*, but merely stand for an object. Similarly in the case of 'effect'. Hartshorne is only able to advocate his case at the expense of converting a general term into a sort of proper name; yet he requires 'cause', 'effect', etc., *not* to be proper names for he has spoken of God as coming under both sides of the basic contraries. For God to come under both sides of the 'basic contraries' *demands* that 'cause', 'effect' and the rest *remain* general terms for, as Geach (1962: ch. 2) has argued, proper names do not come in contradictory pairs and neither do they come in opposite pairs, whereas general terms do. Further, proper names and general terms are absolutely distinct as Frege (1952) in his distinction between 'object words' and 'concept words' makes abundantly clear.

IV

I thus reject Hartshorne's principle of 'dual transcendence' as a means of 'bridging the divide', and as I have rejected the other 'general' or 'over-all' approaches I advocate a 'piecemeal' approach. What has to be engaged upon is an investigation to establish whether, in spite of initial appearances to the contrary, there is indeed a divide to be bridged and this, in turn, can only be established by a detailed analysis of the various attributes of God as specified within Christian tradition. If, upon investigation, there is no such divide, it turns out that we have compossible attributes, then all well and good. And by way of seeking to establish such a thesis we could consider as a starter, for example, William Charlton's recent claim that the notion of a non-material personal creator is a coherent one and that there is 'no incoherence in holding both that God is a person and that he is timeless' (Charlton 1988: 63). However, if upon investigation there is a gulf fixed, the divide is fundamentally unbridgeable, then what we may *not* do is to hold, for example, that there are different and incompatible conceptions of 'God' and yet hold: (a) that we all 'really' mean the same by 'God'; (b) that in spite of these different conceptions, different descriptive meanings, or even 'higher order' meanings, that we are all referring to the same F. Some may wish to hold that our descriptions of God *are* inherently self-contradictory, and *necessarily* so since we are trying to express the inexpressible. I have earlier produced grounds for rejecting the 'inexpressibility' thesis but it might hold that our descriptions of God are inherently self-contradictory and necessarily so, since we are trying to express the inexpressible in that we are trying to *say* what can only be *shown*. God's nature as a transcendent being can only be *shown*, not *said*. The problem here is that we have *already* had to *say* what it is that allegedly can only be shown and have thus contradicted ourselves.

I think therefore that the road we have to travel is the hard piecemeal road but with the assurance that with the help of the Holy Spirit we shall indeed be guided into all truth.[9, 10]

[9] In the last section of his paper Geach raises the serious question of whether worship is in fact being paid to the right God. I concur with him that the question whether worship is in fact being paid to the right God cannot be settled by the argument that since there is only one God no λατρεία can 'fail to reach the right address'. He cites several examples in which this total misdirection of λατρεία is 'practically certain'. From such examples we may glean at least a set of features which are sufficient for any F not being God and necessary for any F being God. Having gleaned this list, however, I think we are still faced with the problem of at least two seemingly incompatible descriptive meanings or uses for 'God', since from the set of features gleaned we discover that some members of the set are compatible with *both* the conception of 'God' as impassible, immutable, atemporal and metaphysically simple *and* the conception of 'God' as a ceaselessly changing, perfectly responsive temporal agent continually interacting with his creatures, and other members of the set (at least one) are compatible with only one of the conceptions. From private correspondence I understand that for Geach there is no problem of accommodating the conception of 'God' as 'a ceaselessly changing, perfectly responsive temporal agent, etc.'; he would simply reject this idea as false. He would hold that the two views, the two conceptions, the two descriptive meanings of which I have spoken *are* incompatible and that one must *choose* (cf. his last paragraph).

[10] I am grateful to the Editor for permission to include in the revised version of this paper some initial responses to some points Professor Geach has raised.

Michael Durrant

I am also much indebted to Professor Geach himself for his valuable comments, both in public and particularly in private correspondence.

Additional note to page 73
Geach rightly emphasizes that St Thomas' discussion of 'simple', 'perfect', 'limitless', 'unchangeable' and 'one' is prefaced by the remark that he is about to tell us the way God *isn't*; and working through St Thomas' treatment of the several items we see how well justified this prefatory remark is. 'Limitless' and 'unchangeable' are negative on the face of it. I agree, and I could write my point as: 'Any being ('Anything') which did not exhibit these characteristics would not be God.' Geach has explained to me in private correspondence that he would not wish to reject the thesis: 'Anything that was not limitless and unchangeable would not be God', but on the question whether knowing this to be true would even partially give us knowledge *de Deo, quid sit*, the answer is still 'No'; and with this I concur. Following Geach's exposition my point about 'simplicity' could be re-written as: 'Whatever is God cannot have this or that sort of inner distinction or complexity which is found in creatures', but once again this would not give us even partial knowledge *de Deo, quid sit.*

Geach's point about 'perfection' is potentially a serious difficulty for my thesis, yet it is one with which I would ultimately concur. There is no such X as perfection *simpliciter*: necessarily perfection is always the perfection *of something or other*. As Geach says, to be perfect is to be a perfect A, where 'A' stands for a general term with some definite content. In the light of my ultimate agreement with Geach I should have to re-write my point as (say): 'Any nature which did not exhibit the feature of being a perfect A (whatever "A" is) would not be God, even though we do not yet know what "A" is in the case of God'; or more correctly as: 'Anything that *was an A*, but not a perfect A would not be God.' (I owe this correction to Geach.)

Geach expresses surprise that I should treat 'one' as expressing an aspect of God's nature and I think he rightly criticizes me on this point. One could certainly not agree with Descartes that the oneness, in the sense of the inseparability, of all God's attributes, *itself* is one of God's attributes. Further, if we take 'one' when said of God to mean the inseparable going together of all God's attributes, then we can raise the nasty question: 'How can we then determine that we have a case of God's attributes *inseparably going together*, if we cannot answer the question: "God is one what?"?' For to be one is always to be one *something or other*, one F (where 'F' furnishes a principle of counting in its own right). I think one has to say with St Thomas and Geach that 'one' *in divinis* does not mean any positive attribute but connotes *indivisio*, there not being one *and* another. In private correspondence Geach has stressed and developed the importance of *not* regarding 'one' as expressing an attribute of God. The declaration in Deuteronomy (vi 4) should be translated as: 'Hear O Israel: YHWH is one God, YHWH *alone.*' In the light of such considerations my point could perhaps be re-written as: 'Any X which exhibited more than one divine nature would not be God; any nature which was found not to be single but many (or more than one) would not be God.' Geach has helpfully suggested that the point could be made thus: 'Any doctrine or story bringing in more than one divine nature has to be false.'

The Meaning of 'God'—II

PETER GEACH

Holding God to be transcendent does not mean having to regard the grammar of the word 'God' as isolated or unique or inscrutable: and in speaking of grammar I use this word in its familiar sense, not in some ill-explained neo-Wittgensteinian sense. I want to make a methodological suggestion. When a sentence containing the word 'God' is puzzling, it may help to look at a grammatically possible replacement for the word. For example, if we wish to understand the statement that God is man's last end, let us consider what it implies to say that gold, or sex, or military glory, is a given man's last end.

I think I agree with Durrant that grammatically 'God' is a common noun. However, even if we regarded 'God' as a proper name, that would not block further questions as to its mode of significance—unless indeed we held something like Mill's view that proper names are 'meaningless marks'. This view has been remarkably durable, but I do not mean to replay just now what I have often said against it; I shall just say I find it inept and perverse.

Durrant alludes to the *Tractatus* doctrine of that which comes out, *sich zeigt*, in our use of language but cannot be described in language. It is very easy to raise objections to Wittgenstein over this that look quite insuperable; but I think further thought shows his doctrine to be far more defensible than Durrant allows. However, it is probably unnecessary to follow this line of thought further at the moment; for by the *Tractatus* doctrine *every* linguistic sign, simple or complex, has features that *sich zeigen* but cannot be described; this would not be a peculiarity of the word 'God'.

The medieval doctrine that we do not know concerning God *quid sit* has given rise to much confused discussion; this is a matter partly of ignorance, partly I fear of an appetite for mystification. If somebody denies that we can know of God *quid sit*, and then goes on to affirm various things about God, this may look like plain inconsistency; but it need not be anything of the sort. Almost any affirmative predication about X may be regarded as answering the question 'What is X?'; but the question *'quid est?'* in Scholastic philosophy, like the Aristotelian *'τί ἐστιν;'* from which it derives, has a much more restricted range of answers. Socrates, for example, is a man, a philosopher, a five-footer, snubnosed, elderly, a son of Sophroniscus, an inhabitant of Athens; all of this would count as telling us things that Socrates is, but by medieval standards only 'Socrates is a man' answers the question *'quid est?'*.

I am not here asking people to treat as firmly established, let alone as obvious, the difference between predications that are, and ones that are not, quidditative or substantial. But neither has anyone the right to take it for granted that this medieval stuff has long since been shown worthless by the labours of John Locke. Let us not forget that John Locke's philosophy of substantial terms led him to deprecate the endeavours of chemists to isolate pure samples of known chemical species and determine their properties. It is on record that the chemists merely found Mr Locke 'prating and troublesome' (Holmyard 1931: 143), and then pursued their researches with success. When Sir John Lockyer gave the name 'helium' to the source of a particular bright line in the Sun's spectrum, he was affirming something of helium, but he did not know of it *quid sit*; we have a much better acquaintance with helium, now that it can be isolated and stored and liquefied. If someone should compare our present knowledge of God to Lockyer's knowledge of helium, he would not be saying something obviously absurd, nor yet refuting himself in every affirmation he made about God.

I find Durrant arguing that since God is said to be 'simple, perfect, limitless, unchangeable and one' we are thereby given at least part of the sense of the word 'God': whatever nature did not exhibit at least these characteristics would not be God. Durrant alludes to St Thomas Aquinas in this context, but St Thomas' discussion of these terms occupies Questions 3 to 11 of Part I of the *Summa Theologiae*, and St Thomas prefaces the discussion by saying he is about to tell us *de Deo quomodo non sit*, the way God isn't (Thomas Aquinas 1964–81: vol. II, 1a. 3). And if we work through St Thomas' treatment of the several items, we see how well justified this prefatory remark is. The terms 'limitless' and 'unchangeable' are negative on the face of it. The question about God's simplicity is answered by St Thomas with a series of denials that God has this or that sort of inner distinction or complexity which is to be found in creatures. 'Perfect' sounds more positive, but a moment's thought shows that there is no such perfection as perfection: we cannot sensibly predicate 'perfect' unless we have in mind a perfect A, where 'A' stands in for a general term with some definite content. After a lecture I gave to first-year students at Leeds, an overseas student gravely rebuked me: 'Professor, in your lecture you spoke of perfect circles. That was very wrong: only God is perfect.' I could not help remembering, though I was too kind to say, that in English (and in several other European languages) the adjective for 'perfect' is often attached to the noun for 'imbecile' or 'idiot'.

I am really surprised that Durrant should treat 'one' as expressing an aspect of God's nature. We may remember that Descartes explains 'one' when said of God as meaning the inseparable going together of all God's attributes. This enables Descartes, so he fancies, to quash a possible objection that his idea of God has no single source, but has been fadged up out of ideas acquired from several sources. Descartes replies that oneness, or the inseparability of all God's attributes, is itself one of God's attributes! It ought not to take any Fregean subtlety of mind to find this fishy. Indeed, long before Frege St Thomas discussed the use of the word 'one' *in divinis* and clearly explained that it does not mean any positive attribute, *non ponit aliquid*, but connotes *indivisio*, there not being one *and* another. The Divine Nature is one; that is, there is not, as the heathen fancied, a divine nature *and* another divine nature (say the natures of Mars and Venus). A Divine Person, say the Holy Ghost, is one; that is, as the Athanasian Creed says, there is only one Holy Ghost not three Holy Ghosts. (cf. Thomas Aquinas 1964–81: vol. VI, 1a. 30, 3)

Much that Durrant says relates to the alleged difference between the God of philosophy and the God of 'the Christian believer'. Right at the outset I find his presentation puzzling. The scriptural presentation of God came long before the disciples were first called Christians. More important, I find it very odd when an 'Anselmian' God is *contrasted* with the God of 'the Christian believer'. Surely people who write this way must be focussing their attention on a few chapters of the *Proslogion* and quite forgetting that St Anselm wrote one of his best-known works to expound and defend what is 'foolishness to the Greeks': that our sins, *quanti ponderis!*, drew the love of God down to birth as a man and death on the Cross. (Anselm 1940–68: vol. II, *Cur Deus Homo*)

I find myself, moreover, simply unable to make the 'thought-experiment' Durrant cites from Morris. I can no more imagine somehow 'discovering' that a being knowledgeable but not omniscient, and in other ways limited, created and sustains the world, than discovering by some New Math. that 3×0 is not 0. (There was a New Math. textbook that actually implied that, but the author had certainly blundered.)

A correspondent once urged me to read the Scriptures more in order to learn better what God is like. I hope I am always willing to learn more from the Scriptures: for the present let me detail some of the things I seem to have learned already. That God *is* from before the Earth and world were made, and for ages without end. That God made all things by his mere word. That God is everywhere and knows all things, in Heaven and Earth and Hell. That God does as he will, and rules in the kingdoms of men, and uses wicked rulers as the tools he will wear out and throw away. That what the pagans ascribe to natural causes are his work; he makes day and night, summer and winter; he feeds the lions who roar after their prey; he forms each child in the womb. That he is not a man that he should lie; he speaks truth and keeps covenant for ever. And much more.

But when I turn from the Scriptures to Greek philosophy I seem to find echoes of much of this. I have specially in mind not Plato, but the pre-Socratic philosophers. I am amazed at the perversity of Christians, with the Torah accessible to them, who comment upon the hugely irrational and immoral legislation of Plato's *Republic* not only without disgust but with a solemn affected admiration. (Plato grew even worse in his old age, when he proposed laws for arresting and brainwashing people to persuade them of his 'proofs' that heavenly bodies were deities; see Plato 1963: *Laws*, Bk X.) But the theology of the early Greek philosophers, though of course mixed with what from a Scriptural point of view are grave errors, contains many valuable dicta. Xenophanes mocked at the manlike, lustful, deceitful gods of tradition, and taught that there is one God, who is all eye, all ear, and all mind, who without toil sways all things by the thought of his mind. Heraclitus writes of a Logos that ever is, ἐόντος αἰεὶ (a Homeric epithet for the immortal gods), and conformably to which everything comes to be, of a wisdom that steers all things. Empedocles writes of a God who cannot be seen or handled, who has no human head, no arms or legs or 'hairy genitals', but is 'a sacred and unutterable thought flashing through the whole world'. Anaxagoras outraged the Athenians by telling them that the Sun was just a red-hot mass and the Moon a lump of earth lit up by the Sun; the world was ruled by a Mind, Νοῦς, which was unaffected by the processes of material change and had complete knowledge and power over all that happens. (See Kirk, Raven and Schofield 1983.) I see no great contrast between all of this and Scriptural descriptions of God.

Of course I know there are those who hold other views both of Hebrew religion and of Greek philosophy. I have in person been assured that the ancient Hebrew religion was a polytheism, with goddesses and all; Moses, I read in a history of Israel, probably worshipped a sacred snake kept in the so-called Ark of the Covenant. To be sure one would get a very different view from the Scriptural histories; but these have undergone drastic redaction by later monotheistic reformers. It would be nice to know how people know all this. On the other side, John Burnet anxiously interprets early Greek philosophy so as to eliminate any hint of theism: for example the Logos of Heraclitus which αἰεί ἐστίν is Heraclitus' own theory, which he regards as *permanently valid*, and of course as having everything *come about in accordance with it*! (Burnet 1930: 133) That is the sort of thing men say; I really cannot argue the matter.

While I by no means wish to confine the knowledge of God to Scriptural revelation, I regard it as a tremendously serious question whether worship is in fact being paid to the right God. The question is not to be settled by the argument that since *there is* only one God, no worship paid as to a God, no λατϱεία, can fail to reach the right address. The argument is a mere paralogism, as is quite easily shown. Here there arises the point of method raised at the beginning of the paper. Let us shift the example from divine worship to political support, and consider an imaginary case I constructed in another piece of work (Geach 1969: 109–10). An unscrupulous canvasser is securing the vote of a man for the candidate sponsored by the Prime Minister, at the relevant time Mr Harold Macmillan. The voter is in a state of senile confusion: he has hopelessly confounded Mr Macmillan with the labour hero Ramsay MacDonald of his own youth, and he associates the noun 'Unionist' not with the Conservative and Unionist Party, but with Trades Unions. Although at the relevant time there was only one Prime Minister, it would be quite unfair to count the old man as a supporter of that Prime Minister. Similarly, if a man has sufficiently misguided religious opinions he cannot count as a worshipper of the only true God: because, as St Thomas puts it, the object of his opinions is not God—*quia id quod ipse opinatur, non est Deus* (Thomas Aquinas 1964–81: vol. XXXII, 2a2ae. 10, 3 ad 3).

I can cite several examples in which this total misdirection of λατϱεία is practically certain:

1. The Pharaoh Akhnaton was a monolatrous worshipper of the Sun. His hymns to the Sun are clear examples of λατϱεία: but the Sun is not God, and indeed for the Jews such worship counted as utter abomination (Deuteronomy iv 19 and xvii 2–5, Job xxxi 26–28, Ezekiel viii 15–16).

2. Many people have recognized λατϱεία in the worship of Krishna. But what should my reaction be to this when I read, as I did in a pamphlet of Hindu propaganda, that although born to a human mother Krishna showed his divine nature by—rogering thousands of women in one night?! 'Can a mere man do this?'

3. In a business call on a man who had some such title as Professor of Religion I noticed on his wall a picture of a female figure with a superfluity of arms: her expression was ferocious, each hand carried a lethal weapon, and she wore a sort of hula skirt of arms severed at the shoulder. 'What a horrible thing!' I exclaimed. 'Don't you realise that for them this represents the Supreme Being?' he replied in a severe tone. 'If that's the representation' I rejoined 'it's not the Supreme Being that is represented!'

4. Any study of the Mormon literature quickly shows that the god they worship is a false god. In fact, they themselves offer a complete

self-exposure when they *attack* worship of the God 'without body, parts, or passions' mentioned in the first of the Thirty-Nine Articles!

5. The Rastafarians worship as god a mythical character based on the late Haile Selassie. People show a curious reluctance to call this religion false, I imagine because they think this is 'racist'; but a religion with hostility to whites written into it is just as viciously false as one involving hostility to blacks.

6. Some people who claim the Christian name believe in a god who is so far from omniscience that his 'beliefs' sometimes turn out to be false; who consequently is liable to nasty surprises from the misconduct of men. In short,

A god of kindred seed and line,
Man's giant shadow, hailed divine.
(Sir William Watson, 'The Unknown God')

I conclude by saying with the Psalmist (cxix 104, 128): I hate every false way. The only true God is the God of truth: God does not contemplate truth from outside, as if in principle the correctness of his thoughts were judgeable for their conformity to a standard ('judgeable by whom?' one might well ask); rather, he constitutes all truth—necessary truth by his nature, contingent truth by his operative or permissive will. The Truth which is God is the goal our minds are made for, otherwise we fail like seeds that never grow to maturity. Any other god is a false god; in particular, a god such as some contemporaries honour, who is so far from constituting the truth that he doesn't even always attain it.

Language, Interpretation and Worship—I

MARTIN WARNER

I

Biblical Interpretation

'There is a kind of eloquence', maintained St Augustine,

> which is manifestly inspired by God. Biblical writers have spoken with this kind of eloquence. . . . [On the other hand] they have uttered some passages with a beneficial and salutary obscurity (*salubris obscuritas*), to exercise and, in a sense, to polish the minds of their readers, to break down aversions and spur on the zeal of those who are anxious to learn, as well as to conceal the meaning from the minds of the impious. (Augustine 1947: IV.6.9; IV.8.22, with one amendment to the translation)

That noted Augustinian, Blaise Pascal, wrote of the Christian Revelation more tersely: 'There is enough light for those who desire only to see, and enough darkness for those of a contrary disposition.' (Pascal 1966: *Pensée* 149) The paradigm of sacred eloquence for Augustine is, of course, that of Christ, and there are echoes here of two Dominical sayings: one is the use of Isaiah vi 9–10 to account for the obscurity of the parables as devices to conceal (Matthew xiii 10–16; Mark iv 11–12; Luke viii 10; see also John xii 37–40); the other is the indication towards the end of the Johannine farewell discourses that so far 'I have said these things (ταῦτα)to you in figures' (ἐν παροιμίαις; 'in dark sayings') though a time is coming when it will be be appropriate to 'tell you plainly (παρρησία) of the Father' (John xvi 25); here the obscurity can more properly be conceived of as 'salutary'. The interpretive difficulties of these passages are considerable, they are indeed themselves 'dark sayings', and I shall return to the more positive one later; but for the present I am concerned merely to note that the double contrast between plain and obscure speech about divine matters and, within the latter, between positive and negative uses of obscurity appears to be inscribed prominently within the foundation documents of the Christian church—it was not just invented by St Augustine.

Nor, indeed, is it an invention of Christianity. The Rabbinic conception of the sanctity of the Torah incorporated both the recognition

Martin Warner

that much is plain to us—'The Torah spoke as human beings do'—and also the midrashic doctrine of 'omnisignificance', that every detail of the text, however obscure, has an importance which we are called to explore—though of course our eyes may be shut as in Isaiah's day (see Kugel 1981: 104). For Christians the issue of the positive uses of the figurative is sharpened by the key role in recorded Dominical teaching of parables (especially in the Synoptics), images and related 'dark sayings' (especially in John); thus it is appropriate that in the passage quoted Augustine should lay more stress on the positive uses of obscurity than the negative. This emphasis is also apparent in his *Confessions* where, in somewhat Rabbinic manner, plainness and obscurity appear to be not just properties of different passages but of the very same portions of Scriptural text: 'while it was easy to read for everybody, it also preserved in the more profound sense of its meaning the majesty of something secret'; this 'more profound sense' was to be sought *'ad sacramentorum'* (Augustine 1963: VI.5).

Setting aside the ramifying complexities attendant upon this last move, we have here the outlines of what may be described as the 'traditional' approach to Scripture (both Christian and Jewish) until the rise of humanistic forms of biblical criticism in the Renaissance, for Augustine was both influential and exemplary. Scriptural writings, it was held, possessed multiple significance, and their characteristic inner dynamic was provided by their providing human form for divine speech—what for Christians was the incarnational principle to be received *ad sacramentorum*. The stylistic mark of this inbreaking of the divine Word has been illuminatingly described by Professor Kugel as 'lawlessness'. Given the secular norms of the reader,

> what was recognizably rhetorical or poetic was attributed to the fact that human beings were the utterers of the Divine Word, or that . . . the Divine Word was framed for human understanding. But all that seemed awkward, unrhetorical, and even incomprehensible was explained by the text's divinity. It was a lawless text, framed by the Lord of all—and 'who shall say to Him, "Do not act so!"' (Job ix 12). . . . It is this stylistic lawlessness which vouchsafes the Bible's Divine character and leads the reader to look more deeply for its hidden significance. (Kugel 1981: 205–6)

Crucial to this approach, of course, is the presupposition that scriptural texts are authoritative. If a secular text contains incomprehensible passages or otherwise transgresses the norms of language or genre this may be a sign of incompetence, even Homer nods. With this move barred we are forced to look elsewhere; thus 'lawlessness' can become a sign of God's intention, and Scripture's religious significance seen to arise from its presentation of discontinuities between the human and divine orders, thereby providing logical space for the procedures of typology and allegory.

There is, however, a catch. The ascription of 'lawlessness' is dependent on the identification of the laws or norms being breached, but those of the reader may be different from those of the writer; what was lawless to Augustine may not have been to Isaiah. This was recognized in the tradition; Augustine remarked on stylistic features to be found in Scripture which were not to be found in the secular paradigms (1947: IV. 20. 41; see also III. 37. 56), and St Thomas was clear that divine inspiration was not to be understood as divine dictation—the prophets chose their own words (Thomas Aquinas 1964–81: vol. XLV, 2a2ae. 172, 3 ad 1, further refs in app. 2; see also vol. I, 1a. 1, 10 and app. 13 and Smalley 1952: 293ff). But the humanistic revolution in exegesis, from which modern biblical research is descended, began the process of using the recognition of this relativity to subvert the religious significance of apparent lawlessness. With the Renaissance the biblical texts came to be seen increasingly, from a stylistic point of view, as 'human creations that . . . differ from our own compositions principally because they were written in another land centuries ago' (Kugel 1981: 206), and the Reformation insistence that the Bible is self-interpreting added to the impetus to make plain apparently obscure speech.

Today we are familiar with readings of biblical texts which attempt to take account of the *Sitz im Leben* of the supposed originals and the literary conventions used by the editors or authors. Where such considerations do not disperse obscurity we can always fall back on our ignorance; 'their world was not our world' remarks the Bishop of Durham (Jenkins 1987: 37), so obscurity is not to be wondered at—indeed, on these accounts the wonder is often that anything is plain at all, but the reason has nothing to do with divine inspiration. Whereas in the older tradition reading the Bible as literature, in terms of secular conventions, was subordinated to reading it as authoritative scripture, today the priority has at the very least been reversed.

The fascinating history of post-medieval biblical exegesis which underpins our present situation is complex and tangled, but one strand is worth picking out for present purposes, since it has a linguistic aspect. Part of the problem with the older tradition was that, at least in the hands of its less creative practitioners, it seemed to attempt to domesticate the *mysterium tremendum et fascinans* with its ramifying rules for figurative interpretation, for according to St Augustine we should in general 'understand as figurative anything in Holy Scripture which cannot in a literal sense be attributed either to an upright character or to a pure faith' (1947: III.10.14); these rules no doubt served 'to exercise and, in a sense, to polish the minds' of the readers of Scripture, but are often reminiscent of attempts to 'draw out Leviathan with a fishhook' (Job xli 1). Conservative exegetes thereby found their position undercut when confronted by the Enlightenment theories about language associated, *inter alia*, with the Royal Society, John Locke and his deist associate Anthony Collins. For Locke, rational uses of language are governed by rules whereby each proposition relates the ideas designated in a determinate manner (1959: vol. II, book III, ch. x, paras 23–9; ch. xi, 26). Collins exploits this approach in his dismissal of allegorical interpretations of the prophets:

> To suppose that an author has but one meaning at a time to a proposition (which is to be found out by a critical examination of his words) and to cite that proposition from him, and argue from it in that one meaning, is to proceed by the common rules of grammar and logic; which, being human rules, are not difficult to be set forth and explained. But to suppose passages cited, explained and argued from in any other method, seems very extraordinary and difficult to understand, and to reduce to rules. (Collins 1737: 45–6; see also Locke 1959: vol. II, book III, ch. ix, paras 22–3 and book IV, ch. xviii, para. 3; for more general discussion see Frei 1974: ch. 4.)

Meaningfulness and intelligibility, it is being none too subtly suggested, presuppose reducibility to human rules; it follows that a 'lawless' text is simply unintelligible. If traditionalists objected that the Bible constituted a falsifying counterexample to the Enlightenment thesis it could be replied that in their practice they did not treat it as genuinely lawless, but as subject to rules of their own licencing multiple significance which were inadequately grounded.

In Collins' hands the new thinking about language served to exclude the possibility of Divine intervention in words as his more general deistic convictions excluded them in deeds; God is squeezed out of yet more of the gaps and divine inspiration excluded from Scripture not only with respect to its reference (the historicity of its narratives), but also to its sense (its alleged multisignificance). Although Collins' particular intellectual underpinnings are now very dated, there are significant twentieth century analogues and the upshot is rather familiar. The Lockean approach to language has affinities with the Enlightenment project of a universal language or 'character' in which each word would relate to a different idea and the syntax be transparent. Leibniz's logical work was in part intended as a contribution to the syntax of the universal character, and although the semantics proved intractable (as, indeed, did the whole 'way of ideas') the logical positivist movement, with post-Leibnizian logical syntax providing the framework within which the verification principle did its semantic work, was its lineal descendant. This principle imposes its own laws and, once again, the penalty of lawlessness is cognitive meaninglessness. Logical positivism is long dead but modern biblical research often seems haunted by its ghost, or by relevantly similar linguistic theories allowing no logical space for the Word to be incarnated in words, which is reinforced by a scepticism about miracles, the historicity of the Biblical narratives and the coherence of the canonical books with which the Deists would have felt at home.

The upshot is that to a very considerable extent the notion of the authority of Scripture has become problematic even for Christians. To understand the texts we need to engage in exercises of historical imagination, identifying the conventions and presuppositions of the writers in so far as they are accessible to us, and inevitably this involves us in some degree of 'placing' and hence judging those norms in relation to our own. So far as conventions are concerned the New Testament writers see the Old Testament as foreshadowing the Christian dispensation and accordingly make significant use of what we call 'types': Jonah's deliverance as a type of Christ's Resurrection, the Red Sea crossing of baptism, Melchizedek of Christ himself and so on (Matthew xii 40, I Corinthians x 1–6, Hebrews vii); the judgment of contemporary Christian scholars on typology is best seen by their own practice in interpreting the Old Testament—it is negative. With respect to presuppositions, the most frequently cited here is probably that of demon possession. The same symptoms that would now be diagnosed as epileptic fit or diabetic coma would in the Palestine of Jesus' day have been understood as demonically inspired, and the treatments most of us would choose today demonstrate our judgment of the ancient diagnosis. The New Testament writers presupposed a world in which demonic possession was prevalent, even the norm in cases of illness, whereas we do not; as Wittgenstein put it of a somewhat similar case: 'We say: these people do not know a lot that we know. And, let them be never so sure of their belief—they are wrong and we know it. If we compare our system of knowledge with theirs then theirs is evidently the poorer one by far.' (Wittgenstein 1969: para. 286)

Attempts are sometimes made to block this conclusion by invoking the notion of cultural totalities, and insisting that the total world view lying behind the New Testament documents, for example, is too alien from our own for such judgment to be possible; in a very strong sense, 'their world was not our world'. But this form of relativism is open to criticism from at least four directions: philosophical, theological, historical and hermeneutic. Philosophically speaking, difference can only be identified where similarity is also discernible, radical conceptual relativism is incoherent (see Davidson 1974); in this instance, to pick out the New Testament background as a totality or 'world' is already to presuppose a considerable amount that is intelligible about it. Theologically speaking, problems are raised if the Scriptures are to be regarded as having contemporary religious significance; the required separation between religious affinity and conceptual discontinuity threatens to to evacuate Christian (and indeed Jewish) theology of distinctive content.

Again, historians may reasonably object that we can find close analogies between first and twentieth century thinking: a writer as close to the Fourth Evangelist's thought world as Philo dismisses belief in demons (and of course exorcism is practised in England and the United States even today); Josephus, like Thucydides before him, appeals to eye witness testimony to support his narratives, as does the author of Acts—and as in modern courts of law—while the related distinction between myth and fact, so widely invoked today, is at least as old as Plato. The Bishop of Durham's claim that the Gospel writers could not have shared 'our concern for our types of either historical or scientific statements' because 'nobody had thought that sort of thing up' (Jenkins 1987: 37), is either so qualified as to be trivial or else historically false. And from the point of view of hermeneutics, the theory and practice of interpretation, we need to remember that cultural artefacts are always read by us in the context of a tradition (see Gadamer 1975), and that in this case it is a tradition that bridges the biblical world or worlds and our own. The patristic and scholastic patterns of allegorical and, indeed, typological interpretation were rooted in the ancient conventions, and our modern ones are in part a product of the principled rejection of those modes by Enlightenment scholars.

Thus much modern biblical research has clear affinities with what Paul Ricoeur has characterized as the 'hermeneutics of suspicion' (1970: I, 2), which put texts to the question in order to 'demystify' them and uncover their presuppositions; ironically, procedures originally developed in the quest to uncover the 'Jesus of history' as a suitable object of faith, lying behind the distorting first century presentation, are in the aftermath of that quest primarily used simply to analyse that presentation. As Nietzsche saw, the tools of philological and historical scholarship have immense subversive potential with respect to our cultural icons, in the religious case pointing to a self-reflexive twist: 'what really triumphed over the Christian god [was] Christian morality itself, the concept of truthfulness that was understood ever more rigorously' (1974: V, 357). Nietzsche's point is important; whether it was indeed the Christian God that was overthrown or merely a deistic idol is open to dispute, but the claim that Christianity cannot renounce that concern with truth which scholarship exemplifies without denying itself has considerable force; in this sense there can be no going back.

However it does not follow that Augustine's claims for the authority of Scripture have been falsified, and here Ricoeur's distinctions are useful: 'The contrary of suspicion, I will say bluntly, is faith. What faith? No longer, to be sure, the first faith of the simple soul, but rather the second faith of one who has engaged in hermeneutics, faith that has undergone criticism, postcritical faith.' (Ricoeur 1970: 28) Ricoeur distinguishes between a 'first' or 'primitive naïveté', which involves an 'immediacy of belief' to which an educated twentieth-century reader cannot with integrity return, and a 'second naïveté in and through criticism' which allows a 'second immediacy'. (1969: Conclusion) The former involves an 'ability to live the great symbolisms of the sacred in accordance with the original belief in them'; Augustine's resort to allegory is arguably an indication that even by the fourth century a 'first immediacy' was no longer available, at least with respect to some of the Old Testament texts, but this did not prevent him from treating them as authoritative. It is a matter of some religious significance whether the way remains open to a hermeneutics of 'postcritical' faith beyond the contemporary hermeneutics of suspicion.

II

Language

The possibility of a hermeneutics of postcritical faith is a matter that needs to be addressed at several levels, and in a number of different contexts. But since theories of language have played a significant role in shaping the issue, any attempt to resolve it must have a linguistic dimension—and it is this that I wish to explore.

Even restricting attention to the linguistic level, there is a wide variety of forms with which one might reasonably associate 'salutary obscurity', and they do not all require the same treatment. As Basil Mitchell has remarked: 'it is all too common to hear words like metaphor, myth, simile, analogy, allegory, parable, symbol, image, model used in theological discussion as if they were entirely interchangeable' (Mitchell 1990: 185). Myth, allegory and parable are all forms of narrative, whereas symbol, model and image characteristically involve non-narrative representation; metaphor and simile are particular uses of language, whereas analogy is a relation which may ground certain uses of language; finer discriminations are of course possible. Nevertheless, in use these categories are often fluid; if the rules associated with the different categories are taken as mutually exclusive and definitive, then Scripture is not alone in being 'lawless'; it is characteristic of the language of imaginative demand that it both employs and breaks open the standard and somewhat static rules of classification.

Many of the Johannine images, for example, have a dynamic aspect: 'I am the door of the sheep' appears to exemplify metaphorical use of a visual image, but its point is given by an incipient narrative ('if any one enters by me, he will be saved'; John x 9); further, it is qualified by being juxtaposed with the visually incongruous but formally similar 'I am the good shepherd' with its own iconographic potentialities, Old Testament resonances (most obviously Ezekiel xxxiv), and a distinctive narrative hinted at by the adjective which in turn it gives content to ('I know my own and my own know me . . . and I lay down my life for the sheep'; John x 14–15)—a narrative contextually pointing to the analogy that grounds the metaphorical image. If Scripture is treated as interdependent, as it is in the imagination of most Christians, then at least two Synoptic parables are evoked (both of which, in different ways, also echo Ezekiel's complex oracle): the man who seeks his lost sheep and rejoices in its finding, a rejoicing that parallels the joy of heaven (Luke xv 3–7; Matthew xviii 12–14) gives further content to what is involved in the good shepherd knowing his sheep; the parable of the sheep and goats (Matthew xxv 31–46) gives a somewhat darker gloss on 'my own know me'. But a further gloss is given in the good shepherd saying itself: 'I know my own and my own know me, as the Father knows me and I know the Father'; in many ways the application of this whole complex to the divine mystery has proved immensely fertile, but it has also been thought necessary to apply certain controls. How is one to relate the goodness of the shepherd to the goodness of God, especially with respect to the dimension of giving one's life for the sheep? Taken one way this seems to invite Patripassianism, which the Church has declared heretical; taken another, the problem finds a form of resolution in orthodox Trinitarian theology. We are close here to Augustine's *salubris obscuritas*; on the one hand the obscurity can conceal, but on the other it can 'spur on the zeal of those who are anxious to learn'; for Augustine, the upshot appears to depend on the spiritual state of the interpreter and he would no doubt claim Dominical warrant: 'my own know me'.

The general problem of the nature of the criteria we should use to sift the creditworthy deliverances of the creative imagination from the delusions of mere fantasy is at least as old as Plato, who was sometimes inclined to take a short way with the issue in a manner analogous to that of the Enlightenment, but never with a good conscience. In Scholastic theology the dynamism of religious parable and image was sometimes combined with the requisite controls, in part, through the distinction between metaphorical and analogical predication. Metaphor breaks free of the standard linguistic rules, for here affirmation is compatible with denial; 'He shall defend thee under his wings, and thou shalt be safe under his feathers' declares the Psalmist (xci 4), and yet one can accept his teaching while denying that the Almighty has feathers—the language is metaphorical. But when we predicate according to the rules of analogy the case is different, for here we are concerned to extend rather than to cancel the meaning of the terms we use; 'He who has seen me has seen the Father' Philip is told (John xiv 9), and in applying the goodness of the good shepherd to our heavenly Father we are using a term which cannot he denied of him without rejecting Jesus' teaching; yet in applying it to him we are extending its use, for God is not subject to the vicissitudes which give sense to the notion of human goodness—but it is extension, not cancellation. Only those metaphorical utterances that are consistent with the affirmation of the authoritative analogical predicates can be accepted, thus God's goodness warrants his presentation under the figure of a shepherd, but not of a wolf.

This approach is, of course, subject to a number of difficulties. First, in St Thomas metaphor applies only part of the literal meaning of a term to a subject, so that one can always cancel the term by reference to the other parts (Thomas Aquinas 1964–81: vol. III, 1a. 13, 9), but one may well query whether this is not to analyse the figurative on the inappropriate model of the literal; if it is, then the whole contrast is suspect. Second, in the case of predication by analogy it needs to be made clear how one is to identify an extension of meaning as an extension, not merely equivocation on the one side or application to an unusual reference range on the other. Third, it needs to be made clear how we are to understand the term in its extended sense and to identify its truth conditions. St Thomas distinguishes between item signified and mode of signification (Thomas Aquinas 1964–81: vol. III, 1a. 13, 3); goodness properly belongs to God but the mode in which it does so is unique, and since human words 'have a way of signifying that is appropriate to creatures' the mode of signification is extended in predications of God. To this it may be queried how far we can separate the mode of signification from that which is signified; if we abstract from the mode in which goodness belongs to men and women what content is left to the claim that God is good? Part of the standard answer is that, as Creator, God is related to us as cause to its effects and, since every primary agent acting according to its nature produces something like itself, our own created nature provides sufficient clues to that of the Creator for the mode in which he possesses his attributes to be at least partially intelligible to us; but of course this reply depends on an Aristotelian account of causality which was swept away in the Enlightenment, along with the associated linguistic theory of multiple signification. In the new intellectual climate it was difficult to see how the linguistic forms I have associated with 'salutary obscurity' could have a significant cognitive function.

In current theories of formal semantics we find sophisticated descendants of the Enlightenment linguistic programme. On these accounts linguistic content is to be identified by a combination of syntax and

Martin Warner

such 'semantic' notions as truth and reference, all of which are precisely rule-governed; no essential reference is required to the use or users of language, the province of what is called 'pragmatics'. An analogous privileging of semantics over pragmatics is to be found in those linguistic theories popular in current literary theory which descend from Saussure, giving priority to *la langue* (the system of linguistic signs) over *parole* (its use). From the point of view of literary criticism a serious weakness of Saussurian linguistics is that it provides no framework for exploring a language's capacity for growth, its creativity, indeterminacy and flexibility, which requires attention to 'the individual speakers within a speech community who provide the point of development of the language in question' (Bell 1988: 27). Similarly, one of the more disappointing characteristics of formal semantics is the logical space it allows for those creative uses of language that involve imaginative demand, such as live metaphor. We do not always find the hostility to 'figurative speeches and allusion' associated with John Locke (1959: vol. II, book III, ch. x, para. 34), but even when it is conceded that the use of metaphors and other figures may have certain cognitively desirable effects they are not regarded as having any intrinsic power of enhancing our understanding; according to one influential theorist: 'Metaphors mean what the words, in their most literal interpretation, mean, and nothing more. . . . What I deny is that metaphor does its work by having a special meaning, a specific cognitive content.' (Davidson 1978; 1984: 245, 262)

There are, I think, general difficulties with those aspects of formal semantics that require a sharp dichotomy between semantics and pragmatics. As David Holdcroft has argued, the identification of communicative behaviour as linguistic requires a theory concerning the 'complicated network of connections between the belief expressed by the speaker's utterance, his beliefs about the context, his belief about the "place" of the utterance in a talk-exchange, and the audience's beliefs' (1981: 196); without such a theory one is in no position to interpret the utterances by ascribing truth-conditions, and without truth-conditions we have no semantics for the language. For these and other reasons it seems appropriate to take account of such 'pragmatic' considerations as communicative capacity, non-linguistic context and utterer's intention in any theory of linguistic meaning, and to make use of the work of those whom Sir Peter Strawson has dubbed 'the theorists of communication-intention' (1969; 1971: 171).

The field here is immensely rich, but for present purposes it may be useful to focus on the possible integration of three types of approach: Paul Grice's notion of implicature, John Austin's account of illocutionary force, and James Ross's portrayal of analogy (though Ross does not strictly fall into Strawson's category). The inferences employed in formal semantics are truth functional; that is, the validity of an inference is a function of the truth conditions of the items inferentially related, so in a valid deductive inference the conclusion cannot be false where the premisses are true; this is the domain of implications, as in classical logic. Implicatures, however, are radically context and relevance dependent and, in the developments of Grice's original project (1975) by psycholinguists, can be graded in terms of strength. To take an example from conversation, if Peter asks Mary 'Would you drive a Mercedes?' and she replies 'I wouldn't drive ANY expensive car', the strongest implicatures are 'a Mercedes is an expensive car' and 'Mary wouldn't drive a Mercedes'—they are necessary to make her response relevant. Rather weaker is 'Mary wouldn't drive a BMW', and if Peter were to reflect that people who would not drive an expensive car would not go on a cruise either and accordingly infer 'Mary would not go on a cruise', he would be at the weakest end of the range of implicatures. On this type of account there need be no cut-off point between assumptions strongly backed by the speaker or writer, and assumptions derived from the utterance but on the hearer's sole responsibility. (Sperber and Wilson 1986: 199) In the case of metaphor,

> in general, the wider the range of potential implicatures the greater the hearer's responsibility for constructing them, the . . . more creative the metaphor. A good creative metaphor is precisely one in which a variety of contextual effects can be retained and understood as weakly implicated by the speaker. The surprise or beauty of a successful creative metaphor lies in . . . condensation, in the fact that a single expression . . . will determine a very wide range of acceptable weak implicatures. (Sperber and Wilson 1986: 236–7)

Such an account may begin to provide a framework within which a cognitive role may be found for indirect discourse, but may also invite the objection that it improperly treats the figurative on the model of the literal, and here Austin's notion of illocutionary force is relevant. The illocutionary act is that which I perform in uttering a locution: stating, promising, assessing, vetoing, apologizing and so on. (Austin 1962). Now on Grice's account (1968) there is an interdependence between what utterers mean by their words and what the words mean according to the public linguistic conventions; when speaking literally the speaker means what he or she says, but with other forms of discourse such as metaphor and irony these elements come apart (Searle 1979); in the case of live metaphors, part of the point of not meaning what one says is to encourage (Warner 1973) or invite (Lamarque 1985) those addressed to imagine or conceive of one item or complex in terms of another, to seek connections, hence the illocutionary force of such metaphors is not what Austin called 'constative' but rather 'hortatory' or 'suggestive';

metaphors are not true or false, but rather apt, unhappy, misleading, illuminating, rich, trite and so on.

If we integrate these two accounts then creative metaphors have the force of inviting one imaginatively to explore an indeterminate complex which is only weakly implicated by the originator, and hence may go beyond what was originally intended. Applied to *salubris obscuritas*, such an account would appear to provide an at least provisional licence for two features of the older tradition. The Augustinian claim that the ability to learn from such obscurity is a function of the spiritual state of the interpreter fits well with the perception that a weak implicatum may be at once appropriate and yet drawn on the hearer's sole responsibility; and the reading of one scriptural section in terms of another, the good shepherd for example in terms of the seeker of a lost sheep, is no longer barred by reference to a supposed original intention. But now it may be objected that we are being altogether too permissive, sponsoring licence in the pejorative sense with an invitation to uncontrolled intertextuality where talk of 'responsibility' is vacuous and reference to reality has dropped out of sight. Traditionally, language about God is taken to be reality depicting because it is used to refer to 'the first cause of things' (Thomas Aquinas 1964–81: vol. II, 1a. 3, 8), all things in general and also in a more specific way of particular religious experiences (Soskice 1985: chaps. 7–8); but the causation in question is certainly non-standard (St Thomas' qualifier 'first' is not there for nothing), and the identification of the universal with the specific cause raises further complexity, quite apart from the problem of identifying which experiences are privileged without reverting to intertextuality; considerations which may give rise to the suspicion that the notion of 'cause' is itself figurative. The problem the traditional doctrine of analogical predication was designed to solve remains pressing.

Ross's portrayal (1981) of the analogy phenomena provides a radical revision of the classical account which appears to serve some of its functions through giving a principled account of the way language is polysemous, allowing us in discourse to generate an indefinitely large number of possible senses of words and other expressions. If the affinities and oppositions for two uses of a term used in literal discourse are different there are two different or analogous meanings; now terms can take on such differences as a result of the words they are combined with and where this happens we have typical uses of the analogy phenomenon which operates throughout language. The networks of analogy that allow us, for example, to drop stitches, friends, and hints without merely equivocating over the word 'drop' put in serious doubt the possibility of constructing a lexicon, with all the ramifications of meaning each word may have, that would fit into a classical truth-conditional theory for a natural language. Complications arise where the analogous extensions are metaphorical, for here 'the originating source of the analogy and the appropriate disanalogy need to be jointly considered' as when it is said of an aging actress with respect to theatre managements: 'She had been *dropped* and the crash splintered the fragile structure of her ego'; in such cases 'many of the affinities and oppositions are carried along in the transfer of meaning' (Kittay 1987: 149–56; see also Ross 1981: 109–19).

Key concepts here are those of context, inertia and force. Some types of utterance are so associated with a particular range of contexts that their utterance in an apparently different one drives the hearer to reinspect the current context or to reinterpret the utterance; linguistic inertia leads one to attempt to construe the words according to the standard patterns, but when the verbal or other context renders such construals unacceptable, the phenomenon of linguistic force comes into play to force adaptations of meaning—metaphor and irony being prime examples. Now in some cases skill in action may be necessary for a full grasp of the discourse, it is 'craftbound', and here the basic vocabulary is anchored to 'benchmark' situations; since 'religion is taught to modulate living . . . and living in God . . . is the object of the craft of Christian doing' (Ross 1981: 167) it too is craftbound, and here scriptural stories act as benchmarks, able to 'structure and stabilize the central meaning relationships' (158). On this account the intertextuality of religious discourse is broken by the relation to practice, and nothing bars treating certain benchmark stories (of the crucifixion and resurrection for example) as having extra-linguistic reference; further, by providing the anchors of benchmark situations and sentences sufficient content is given to the notion of initial context for linguistic inertia to have a role to play in providing controls on scriptural interpretation and perhaps even on the development of doctrine. Figurative language is not unprincipled, for it can be understood as an extension of familiar linguistic phenomena which can be given a law-like mapping in terms of a coherent semantic-cum-pragmatic framework.

Any serious attempt to weave these different linguistic strands together will require us to vary the classical truth-conditional account of meaning as a function from sentences to possible states of affairs by considering context fully.[1] Such a move blurs the semantics/pragmatics

[1] Such integration may also help resolve some well-known difficulties with the analysis of implicature. Grice's insufficiently nuanced account of what it is to 'say', as distinct from to 'implicate', something (see, for example, Travis 1991) can be greatly enriched by use of Ross's account of linguistic inertia anchored by benchmarks. This account also provides a notion of initial context rather more plausible than the assumption of initially undifferentiated data which underlies Sperber and Wilson's 'Principle of Relevance', in terms of which they attempt to unify Grice's Principles of Conversation and to grade the strength of implicatures (Sperber and Wilson 1986: 46–50, 123–132; see also Cooper 1991: 6).

distinction and integrates style with meaning—making, for example, metaphor appear to be both inevitable and ineradicable. In metaphors the normal linguistic meanings of the words used are not cancelled, but the normal contexts standardly presupposed for their application are here clearly not presupposed; the force of the metaphor is to invite the reader or hearer to see the appositeness of the application despite the fact that the context of application is apparently inappropriate, and the need to render such a context relevant forces meaning adaptations—with concomitant implicature shifts—from the norm. Again, the interplay between force and inertia helps us to understand creativity and growth in language; its impersonal aspects, such as those provided by the stereotypic benchmarks, interrelate with the more personal in a creative manner, thus enabling new imaginative achievements to expand and modify the capacity of the language in question—and indeed of those others into which it is translatable. Further, recognition of the phenomena of implicature serves both to remind us that the notion of 'inertia' should not be taken too literally, and to point to the way that language can involve us in forms of holistic understanding—which may place some controls on one's wrestling with Augustine's *salubris obscuritas*.

III

Worship

The practice of worship sharpens the issues about the interpretation of religious texts I raised in the first section of this paper, and provides a suitable field of application for the linguistic considerations I have sketched in the second.

Most Christian worship has a verbal dimension, and the words used are characteristically 'a tissue of scriptural allusion' (Frost 1973: 11) or direct quotation, whether in liturgical or extempore contexts. But the attitude of worship appears incompatible with sitting in judgment on the object of worship, and while authentic response to the numinous may well involve a sense of the inadequacy of words, to the extent that scriptural language is accepted as providing a norm it is regarded as having an at least approximate appropriateness in expressing the relationship between worshipper and God. In other words, biblical language plays an authoritative role in one of the central activities of faith, where the attitude of suspicion can be no more than secondary. But if the authority of that language is subverted this puts in question the activity itself; on such an account it would appear that the Christian's life of prayer and worship is dependent on forms of thought and language which cannot bear critical scrutiny. For Augustine there was no problem; we humbly use forms provided for us in Scripture which are 'inspired by God', and allow our spiritual lives to be nurtured and transformed by them. Humility, however, is not the leading characteristic of the hermeneutics of suspicion.

Claims for the 'lawlessness' of Scripture, as we have seen, could sometimes be undermined by the recognition that the conventions of the writers were not all shared by the readers; where such considerations are applied to the verbal formulations of worship the consequences can be wide-ranging. Leslie Houlden, for example, has objected to use of 'the old purely historical-cum-mythological approach' in modern liturgical formulations (1974: 173) such as we find in the prayer that speaks of Jesus as: 'your living Word: through him you have created all things from the beginning, and formed us in your own image'. Were such language, echoing the first and last books of the Bible as well as the Fourth Gospel, to be barred from Christian worship a significant change would be made in the worshippers' sense of self-identity. Thus Geoffrey Wainwright (1980: 508) replies to Houlden that 'liturgy is a public act by which the worshippers identify themselves with a continuing community and enter into the "myth" of that community'. *Lex orandi*, *lex credendi*; changes of such magnitude in the authorized forms of public worship could hardly fail to have significant consequences for the nature of Christian faith itself.

Worship as such is concerned to express the numinous and our response to it; typically it involves praise of the focus of worship which is conceived as transcending any particular manifestation, and often also involves ritual which both expresses the superiority to the worshipper of the focus of worship and participates in or sustains its power (see Smart 1972: part I). These very general features are sometimes called 'archetypal'. Now in the Judaeo-Christian tradition the visions of Isaiah (vi 1–8) in the Temple and Ezekiel (i; see also x) in exile beside the river Chebar represent classic expressions of the experience of the numinous, thereby providing two of the more important benchmarks for language expressing God's holiness; the Book of Revelation (iv–v) develops the Old Testament models in a distinctively Christian fashion, though with notorious 'obscurity' however 'salutary'. Where there are prescribed forms of worship, typically they use forms of words designed to make the archetypal patterns as expressed through the benchmarks accessible to the worshippers for, to use Mgr Crichton's formulation, 'the aim of the whole [Christian] liturgy is entrance into communion with God, a communion in the divine life and love that constitute the Trinity' (Crichton 1980: 19). Thus Fr Hugo Rahner (1955: 152–5) argues that from Classical times the Christian 'mysteries' as focussed in ritual have involved a principled blend of 'common archetypal elements', Revelation and cultural borrowings; the arche-typal elements are those relating to all worship, Revelation provides the distinctively Christian contribution to liturgy, while cultural borrow-ings are capable in principle of rendering it culturally accessible and relevant. There are many diverse possibilities of tension between these three elements, and the issue raised by Houlden is concerned in the first instance with the relation between the last two—between Revelation and contemporary culture.

One way of resolving the problem, of course, is simply to take contemporary culture as normative in high Deistic manner. If the language and presuppositions of supposed Revelation have been ren-dered unusable through the hermeneutics of suspicion we should sim-ply use those elements of today's culture with which we are in sympathy to give expression to those archetypal elements of worship we feel we can make our own; such tendencies have been familiar from the French Revolution's cult of the Supreme Being to contemporary 'New Age' spirituality. Even in their own terms, however, the (often double) subjectivity involved provides a degree of tension with the demands of transcendence and authority that the 'archetypal' experience of the numinous typically involves; the provision of authoritative benchmarks from beyond the horizon of our own subjectivity appears to fit better with the dynamic of the archetypal elements themselves—which point to transcendence of self, of culture and, indeed, of fully intelligible categories. On the account of language I have sketched such an aspiration cannot be dismissed as simply *un*intelligible.

Houlden, however, does not propose anything so radical. His con-cern is rather that changing conventions and presuppositions change implicatures. Those who attempt to increase cultural accessibility, through the provision of contemporary liturgical forms to replace the sixteenth and seventeenth century models, need to look very carefully at the retention of biblical (and patristic) elements:

> It seems to be deemed sufficient to make liturgical forms virtually catenae of biblical words and images. . . . There has been little sign of any serious attempt to consider whether these words and images still carry their former vividness or are intelligible expressions of what is to be said. Nor is there much sign of awareness of the echoes and contexts of biblical allusion. (Houlden 1974: 173)

The accuracy of this charge is not my present concern, but rather its assumptions about language. The highlighting of the importance of 'echoes and contexts' for the intelligibility of words and images fits well with the account I have given, but two qualifications should be entered. First, to treat scriptural passages or images as authoritative may not be to commit oneself to first-century categories, for those passages may themselves in their own terms be 'lawless', using the dynamism of linguistic 'force' to press the imagination to transcend those categories, and our relative detachment from these may be in some ways beneficial; Houlden objects to 'the old purely historical-cum-mythological approach', but 'purely' is perhaps incautious. Second, and relatedly, we should take into account the ways that successive generations of the 'continuing community' of Christians have used and adapted the 'biblical words and images' in their different cultural contexts; the ancient forms have gathered round them 'echoes and contexts' which are not merely biblical or patristic, affecting our understanding of such expressions as 'living Word', 'from the beginning' and 'formed us in your own image'; if contemporary cultural perceptions do more than force further stepwise linguistic shifts, this needs to be shown.

But this invocation of tradition raises a matter of some theological and hermeneutic delicacy, relating to the Dominical 'dark sayings' with which I began. 'I have said these things to you in dark sayings; the hour is coming when I shall no longer speak to you in dark sayings but tell you plainly of the Father' (John xvi 25); how are we to understand this promise? With one possible exception, discussed in the next paragraph, John does not record Jesus telling the disciples of the Father again, but earlier we have been told both that 'when the Spirit of truth comes, he will guide you into all the truth' (xvi 13) and, apparently in relation to the coming of that same Spirit, that 'I will not leave you desolate; I will come to you' (xiv 18); after the Resurrection Jesus breathes on his disciples saying 'Receive the Holy Spirit' (xx 22). The inference appears to be that Jesus is identifying himself with the Spirit who will tell plainly of the Father, and to the extent that the Holy Spirit remains with his disciples they will be led into all truth. This did not lead St Paul, however, to eschew figurative language in his Epistles, and for all his combination of deep understanding and faith in the power of the Holy Spirit St Thomas still quotes Gregory the Great with approval: 'stammering, we echo the heights of God as best we can' (Thomas Aquinas 1964–81: vol. II, 1a. 4, 1). Whatever being told 'plainly' may mean it does not appear to involve being given words that meet the Enlightenment canons. If we note, however, that this promise represents a response to the difficulty the disciples have been having in understanding Jesus, in part with respect to his self-identification with the Spirit (xvi 16–19), we may begin to suspect that the promise is itself something of a dark saying, and that the resolution of the disciples' puzzlement will be through transforming their understanding rather than simplifying the language, pointing to the Augustinian claim that one's ability to learn from 'salutary obscurity' is a function of one's spiritual state.

But John is an ironist, and he records as part of the same saying in which telling 'plainly of the Father' is placed in the future a declaration to which the disciples reply: 'Now you are speaking plainly, and not παροιμίαν.' (xvi 29) The words in question are: 'I came from the Father and have come into the world; again, I am leaving the world and going to the Father.' They need to be seen in relation to the disciples' earlier puzzlement when Jesus speaks of his 'going': Thomas' 'We do not know where you are going; how can we know the way?' (xiv 4) and the more general 'What is this that he says . . . "because I go to the Father"?' (xvi 17). By having the language that had been 'dark' put in the context of 'coming into' and 'leaving' 'the world' it appears to the disciples that all is now plain. To some extent they show that they have gained in understanding ('By this we believe that you came from God' (xvi 30)); the broadened context has forced linguistic adaptation from Thomas' understanding of the words for 'go', but unconsciously so that their increased understanding is put down to a change in the linguistic status of Jesus' words. However, their understanding is far from complete, and the saying hardly 'plain'. To the extent that Jesus' imminent 'going to the Father' involves leaving the world through death the disciples can hardly be described as prepared for it, Peter attempting to save his master through swordplay (xviii 10). And in the Johannine discourses 'the world' (ὁ κόσμος) is a highly complex notion, as can be seen from Jesus' response: 'I have overcome the world' (xvi 33); coming into and leaving 'the world' are not just equivalent to birth and death—indeed, we are to find that after both death and resurrection Jesus has still 'not yet ascended to the Father' (xx 17).

Whichever words are used (and John moves between ὑπάγω, with its associations of leading others by stages, and πορεύομαι with its reflexive nuance of the middle voice) the notion of 'going to the Father' appears to be one which can seem 'plain' but invites, for one who would interpret 'faithfully' in humble submission to the authority of Scripture, an Augustinian 'exercise' of the mind inspired by the 'zeal' of the Spirit of truth who, in the Dominical words, 'will take what is mine and declare it to you' (John xvi 14), leading the disciple from one range of meaning to another. That such considerations may be relevant to worship is suggested by the close of the *Book of Common Prayer* Exhortation which opens the Orders for Morning and Evening Prayer:

> Wherefore I pray and beseech you, as many as are here present, to accompany me with a pure heart, and humble voice, unto the throne of the heavenly grace.

Language, Interpretation and Worship—II

PETER LAMARQUE

I

Martin Warner's subtle and far-reaching synthesis of philosophical theology and philosophy of language belongs in a cluster of papers he has written on related topics (Warner 1985, 1990a, Introduction to 1990b) so it would be helpful to begin by setting out this wider context. His concerns overall cover three interlocking subjects: biblical interpretation, biblical translation, and reform of the liturgy. All pose a central conundrum, which in its briefest formulation is just this: what kind of meaning is involved in each case? Warner's particular focus is on the role of distinctions like content and style, truth and connotation, literal and figurative, ultimately semantics and pragmatics.

His main polemical point is that we get an intolerably distorted view of all three topics if we come to them with too narrow a conception of meaning, a conception he thinks has been predominant at least since the Enlightenment. It centres on the idea of a core, literal meaning, a cognitive content, isolatable from particular modes of linguistic expression, to a large extent context-independent, and yielding, as it were, some essential message being conveyed. This conception of significant content is associated in early versions with Lockean ideas and the 'universal characteristic', in later versions with truth or verification conditions. Its paradigm not surprisingly is found in scientific writing (at least of a certain kind) where the very same content can be expressed in different ways, can be translated into different languages and can be subject to reasonably clear criteria of testability.

If the Bible and the liturgy could indeed yield such a core content of meaning then the tasks of interpretation, translation and reform would be clearly defined: the interpreter should identify this content, the translator should reproduce it in other languages and the reformer, in the case of the liturgy, should find alternative, perhaps more contemporary, ways of expressing it.

But it seems plain enough, as Warner shows, that this conception of meaning is totally inadequate in all three applications. Warner's proposal is that we abandon the scientific paradigm and adopt instead the paradigm of the creative poetic metaphor as the model of biblical and liturgical meaning. The idea is not in itself new but the novelty resides in Warner's own account of what this paradigm entails. We will return to that in a moment. Why is the Enlightenment conception inadequate?

First of all the demands of the liturgy, involving, in Warner's words, 'the combination of a "vertical", Godward movement with a "horizontal", communal one' (1990a: 154), make the principles of revision enormously complex. Forms of worship must conform both with the spiritual requirement of communion with God, drawing inevitably on biblical archetypes, and also with the imaginative requirements of the community of worshippers, reflecting their own concerns and values. To give attention in the revision of liturgy merely to a putative cognitive content independent of its precise linguistic expression, indifferent to its contextual resonances in the Bible, and insensitive to the imaginative capacities of its users, would be manifestly inadequate if not simply unintelligible.

Equally complex are the demands of the biblical translator. Here the question of style and content is especially acute because it seems at least coherent to mark that distinction within translation (as it probably is not in the case of the liturgy). In the Preface to the *Good News Bible* the distinction is drawn between 'ascertaining as accurately as possible the meaning of the original' and 'express[ing] that meaning in a manner and form easily understood by the readers' (quoted in Warner 1985: 158), the assumption being that the meaning is something apart from its mode of expression. But a look at particular cases soon shows the difficulty of establishing where content ends and style begins. How should we account, for example, for the differences between the following (from Warner 1985: 153–4)?

(1) And the light shineth in darkness; and the darkness comprehended it not. (St John's Gospel, i 5; *Authorised Version*)
(2) The light shines on in the dark, and the darkness has never quenched it. (*The New English Bible*, 1st edition)
(3) The light shines on in the dark, and the darkness has never mastered it. (*The New English Bible*, 2nd edition)
(4) The light shines in the darkness, and the darkness has never put it out. (*Good News Bible*)

or between:

(1) In the beginning was the Word, ... (St John's Gospel, i 1; *Authorised Version*)
(2) When all things began, the Word already was. (*The New English Bible*)

Warner offers perceptive observations as to what is at stake in such variations and his general conclusion is that the whole debate about translation is misconceived if pursued exclusively in terms of content and style. We must ask, he says, not about strict synonymy, certainly not about identity of truth-conditions, but rather whether the translations make the same, or similar, *imaginative demands* as the original and whether they conform to the same *contextual cues* (the latter highlighted in the second example in its putative connection with the opening of Genesis).

That brings us back to interpretation, which is the principal topic of the current paper. Here the focus is on the peculiar kind of difficulty or obscurity—the 'lawlessness' (Kugel), the 'dark sayings' (St John), the 'salutary obscurity' (Augustine)—found in biblical writings. Early interpreters attributed this special difficulty to the Bible's divine character, the 'Word incarnated in the word'. But this idea does not fare well under the conception of meaning as determinate literal content. Post-medieval interpreters sought ways to 'naturalize' the difficult passages, explaining them—even explaining them away—in human or historical terms. Thus, on a good gloss, the 'salutary obscurity' might be broken down into significant content and extraneous ornament, while on a more harsh reading it might be dismissed as merely incomprehensible, a confusion of mind in the human authors. Warner's efforts are directed at giving a more sympathetic account of biblical 'lawlessness', an account which at least finds 'logical space' for the idea that there might be some special religious, or scriptural, significance to it.

II

Warner takes the creative metaphor as paradigmatic in accounting for the peculiar obscurities of some biblical writing. This is not, though, a commitment to viewing the writing as itself metaphorical; it is only a means of characterizing a mode of interpretation. I take it to be a further merit of the proposal that it does not involve a decision in advance on that notoriously difficult question of which passages in the Bible are to be 'taken literally' and which assigned a metaphorical or figurative reading. In effect that distinction is as much under dispute as that between content and style. At best, if I understand Warner correctly, we need only identify those passages which pose special problems for interpretation and translation and those that do not; and that line might be drawn in different places at different times.

Warner's account of creative metaphors goes like this:

> creative metaphors have the force of inviting one imaginatively to explore an indeterminate complex which is only weakly implicated by the originator, and hence may go beyond what was originally intended. (102)

111

Peter Lamarque

The account combines the pragmatic notions of illocutionary force and implicature, making metaphor a feature of context-dependent utterances rather than of sentences or expressions in a language. It identifies metaphor primarily as a phenomenon of communication, defined in terms of communicative intentions and conventionally determined responses. It makes no commitment to the idea that metaphors must yield a determinate literal paraphrase and locates the assessment of metaphor not as a matter of truth and falsity but one of aptness and effectiveness.

Being in broad sympathy with this approach (Lamarque 1982, 1985), I will not say much about it as a theory of metaphor. The more pressing question is how it fares as a paradigm on the three subjects of biblical interpretation, biblical translation and the language of worship. Certainly it offers some immediate advantages over the more restricted conception of meaning defined in verificationist or truth-conditional terms. It highlights the 'imaginative demands' of interpretation, it does justice to the idea of fine-grained distinctions of connotation, it allows for constraints in translation beyond those of literal content, and it points to ways in which biblical obscurities might be cognitively rewarding.

But it remains debatable whether this is the right model for making sense of the peculiar scriptural dimension of the Bible, the idea that the obscurities of meaning might have a divine origin, the 'Word incarnated in the word'. I will outline my doubts on the matter first by looking at some internal difficulties for the proposal, relating to communication, intention and truth, then by putting forward a more radical alternative which supplants the metaphorical paradigm altogether.

The first doubt centres on the appropriateness of the communication or conversational model, which is at the core of the Gricean notion of implicature. It is one thing to account for metaphor *per se* in terms of utterances and communicative intentions relating to speakers and audiences in specific contexts. But does this carry over to the biblical application? Part of the problem, in the biblical case, is simply the remoteness of writer and reader, at least for modern interpreters. It is difficult to reconstruct the shared communicative context.

Certainly it would seem highly implausible to seek a role for Grice's Co-operative Principle and conversational maxims in the generation of biblical implicatures (Grice 1989). In fact this mechanism seems redundant not only in the biblical case but even in the explanation of metaphors in general. The invitation to pursue comparisons and associative networks imaginatively can (*pace* Grice) be recognized contextually without even implicit recourse to conversational principles. In effect, Warner's own supplementary proposal, adapted from Ross, with its appeal to context, inertia and force (103) to explain the motivation behind seeking a metaphorical interpretation for biblical obscurities, shows that conversational principles are not needed. Indeed it is within the spirit of his account to say that the very conventions of biblical exegesis dictate this mode of imaginative response.

Is the notion of implicature itself redundant in Warner's account? I suspect it is, even though he takes as his model not Grice but the sub-Griceans Sperber and Wilson, who replace the conversational maxims with a general principle of relevance in communication and who themselves weaken the original notion of an implicature (Sperber & Wilson 1986). Just how far Warner has moved from the Gricean communication/implicature paradigm comes out in the further problem of what status to ascribe to authorial intentions in biblical interpretation. This reveals a tension in Warner's account for, on the one hand, he favours the framework of pragmatics where context, intention and response are predominant while, on the other hand, he does not wish to be tied to a biblical version of the Intentional Fallacy. To this end he invokes the notion of a 'weak implicature', as defined by Sperber and Wilson, which loosens the link between speaker's intention and licenced inference. The idea represents a significant departure from the original Gricean paradigm. Grice's notion of a conversational, as opposed to a conventional, implicature rests on the idea of an audience working out what a speaker could have meant or intended to convey when in apparent breach of a conversational maxim. The speaker's intention, on this paradigm, forms a constraint on the success of the inferential process. Any loosening of this constraint correspondingly loosens the conversational or communicative basis for implicature. In one respect this is all to the good, given that the conversational paradigm, as we have seen, sits uncomfortably with the biblical application. But the problem of intention remains especially acute in this context. After all, the project is to give some sense to the idea of the 'Word incarnated in the word'; even if the human authors' intentions can be bypassed or overridden that cannot be so with God's intended meaning.

St Augustine had his own subtle route through the problem. He was willing to concede that competent interpretation of the Bible might yield meanings not intended by its human authors. But if these meanings could be shown to be truly consistent with the rest of Scripture then they could be attributed to the intention of the Divine Author who 'foresaw that this very meaning would occur to the reader or listener' (Augustine 1947: III.27.38).

The pragmatic analysis of metaphor—in terms of utterance and illocutionary force—makes reference to a speaker's intentions inescapable. It is helpful, therefore, to distinguish two kinds of intention in relation to metaphorical utterance: what might be called the *con-*

stitutive intention, common to all metaphors, explained in terms of illocutionary force, and what might be called *context-specific* intentions, which relate to the particular communicative purposes of metaphorical usage case by case. Speakers create metaphors to invite a special kind of imaginative response (thinking of one thing in terms of another) but that is rarely an end in itself; further purposes sometimes include the conveying of a particular belief or sentiment or perspective or vision which the speaker wants to share, sometimes the metaphor will be intended as a mere ornament or embellishment or *jeu d'esprit*, sometimes it might have a specific rhetorical purpose, to persuade, to soften, to make a joke.

If it is right that metaphors are governed by these two kinds of intentions then the appeal to 'weak implicatures' will not suffice to remove authorial intention altogether and the model of atomistic communication (individual communicative acts governed by context-specific purposes) will still be predominant. Again, this does not seem the right model for biblical interpretation.

Pragmatic accounts of metaphor which fail to acknowledge both kinds of intentions are in danger of running into further trouble over the perennial problem of the *cognitive* functions of metaphor, or more specifically the use of metaphors to convey beliefs or propositions assessable as true or false. Warner's concern in this paper is primarily with meaning rather than truth and his passing remark that 'metaphors are not true or false, but rather apt, unhappy, misleading, . . .' (102) etc. is meant, I take it, more as a gloss on the 'invitational' analysis than a final statement on the relation between metaphor and truth. But the question of truth and belief cannot be completely detached from the problems posed by Augustine's *salubris obscuritas*; after all, Augustine's discussion is in the context of exploring the relation between *sapientia* and *eloquentia*. That the obscure passages contain wisdom as well as eloquence Augustine never doubted.

Perhaps, though, we can bring Warner's position into line with Augustine's by saying this on behalf of pragmatic analyses of metaphor: that the conveying of truth is not a constitutive aim of metaphor (as it is, say, of assertion) but it can nevertheless be a context-specific aim. Again, the truths conveyed might or might not be explicitly held in mind by the speaker. Sometimes a speaker will indeed want to impart a determinate belief by means of a metaphor; sometimes, though, an audience will be led to entertain, even come to believe, a proposition, not previously considered by the speaker, as a consequence of pursuing the interpretive process. We might be more inclined to think of the truth as contained in the metaphor in the former rather than the latter case.

The question of truth comes up in a more perplexing manner in relation to Warner's appeal to 'benchmark situations'. The conception comes from Ross who defines the notion in terms of meaning. Benchmark situations—and correspondingly benchmark sentences—'anchor' the basic vocabulary of a discourse or mode of discourse and serve to 'structure and stabilize the central meaning relationships' (Ross 1981: 158). A benchmark situation, which might for example be a biblical story, 'provides a stereotype, a paradigmatic case, that fixes the sense of a predicate . . . used to construe it' (Ross 1981: 212). Warner appeals to the notion as a further constraint on the imaginative processes associated with metaphorical interpretation. The idea seems to tie in with a point in Augustine, also on interpretive constraints: 'When we are trying to search out those passages that are obscured by figurative words, we may either start out from a passage which is not subject to dispute, or, if it is disputed, we may settle the question by employing the testimonies that have been discovered everywhere in the same Scripture'. (Augustine 1947: III.28.39) But that highlights a deeper problem for the benchmarks. The notion of 'a passage which is not subject to dispute' presumably cannot—in these days of Ricoeur's 'postcritical faith'—be treated with quite the equanimity displayed by Augustine. If the benchmark situations (and sentences) are to help fix meanings then their own meanings must be stable and determinate. And part at least of what it is to understand their meaning must be to have a conception of the conditions under which they are true.

However, even more seems to be required of the benchmarks in Warner's project over and above the determination of truth-conditions. For Warner wants to find 'logical space' for the idea that Scripture is 'authoritative', that the 'lawlessness' of its writing can have a divine origin. This seems to require not merely a recognition of the truth-conditions of the benchmark sentences but also some kind of acknowledgment of their *truth*. This is particularly apparent in the applications of benchmarks to worship. Without the authority of Scripture, worship, 'one of the central activities of faith' (104), is itself undermined. But that authority resides not merely in meaning but also in truth.

Warner discusses the matter in more detail elsewhere through the example of the expression of penitence in revised forms of worship (Warner 1990a: 161–3). One relevant benchmark here is the vision of Isaiah in the Temple. Isaiah's experience of awe in the face of God—'Woe is me for I am undone; . . . I am a man of unclean lips and I dwell in the midst of a people of unclean lips . . .'—is paradigmatic and as such, on Warner's view, helps constrain implicatures in liturgical expressions of penitence. But when beliefs change, for example concerning the notions of sin and guilt, and expressions of penitence are accordingly toned down, what becomes of the benchmark? Either its authority in determining the scope of implicatures is weakened or it itself must be re-interpreted. Clearly changes in belief (what is taken to be true) and changes in meaning, even at the level of style and implicature, are inextricably bound together.

All this makes the appeal to benchmarks problematic. Basically it is now unclear what kind of constraint they can offer on the imaginative exploration of biblical metaphors (images, parables, etc.). Warner admits that the benchmark passages 'may themselves in their own terms be "lawless"', and also that 'we should take into account the ways that successive generations of the "continuing community" of Christians have used and adapted the "biblical words and images" in their different cultural contexts' (106–7). But that seems to place the benchmark stories in much the same category as the *salubris obscuritas* that they purport to illuminate.

One final observation on the benchmark situations. Warner's use of these as norms in biblical interpretation is not quite the same as Ross's. Ross sees them as constraints on 'craftbound discourse'. But religious language is craftbound in a much broader sense than the language of the Bible itself might be thought of as craftbound. Ross is primarily concerned, in this context, with the meaning constraints on predicates applied to God (love, wisdom, knowledge, power, etc.); his central question is whether such predicates are used equivocally of God and man, and if so whether that leads to non-cognitivism in theology. But his concern is not limited to the appearances of the predicates in the biblical texts. Warner, by contrast, wants the benchmark sentences drawn from the Bible to help illuminate non-benchmark sentences elsewhere in the Bible. And that, I think, is where the problem of a potential circularity comes in.

III

Much of my commentary thus far has been concerned with the internal details of Warner's proposed synthesis. The criticisms have been directed not at the conceptions themselves drawn from philosophy of language but at their application to specific issues relating to biblical interpretation. But now a deeper difficulty with the project begins to suggest itself: perhaps theories of language reach their limit in the context of certain kinds of application. The age-old question of what kind of meaning might attach to *sacred texts* or to worship conceived as *communion with God* is not problematic on the grounds of some mysterious ineffability of the subject matter but rather because theories of meaning are of necessity generalisable and yet certain linguistic phenomena—including, I suggest, those at issue—possess essential features *sui generis*. Take the concept of metaphor. Any adequate theory of metaphor must be able to accommodate the purpose and function of metaphor in a wide range of contexts; if metaphors appear in science or poetry or law or religion the theory should have something substantive to contribute to an understanding of these different applications. And so, I believe, does the theory offered by Warner in the context of biblical interpretation and the liturgy. Yet the theory reaches its limit at the very point where it hopes to be at its most illuminating.

Warner is faced with a dilemma. His project is to try and resist the inclination—predominant since the Enlightenment—to 'naturalize' the obscurities of Scripture, to explain them (explain them away) in human or historical or cultural terms. He does not want a theory of language alone to eliminate the very idea that they might, as Augustine thought, be explicable in scriptural terms, as products, say, of divine inspiration. Yet at the same time he wants to see whether the scriptural dimension could itself be explicable through the resources of a theory of language. So far there might be a tension, but no contradiction. The threat of contradiction comes in the fact that his rejection of the naturalizing tendencies of his opponents takes the form of an explanatory appeal to linguistic phenomena—illocutionary force, implicature, etc.—all of which have paradigmatic non-scriptural, and thus naturalistic, applications. At the very point where the sacredness of the texts is being defended it appears to have been forsaken.

My own proposal is to retain many of the core elements of Warner's account—'imaginative demand', illocutionary force, context dependence, a weakening of the style/content distinction—but change the paradigm and move away from the atomistic conception of meaning conceived in terms of individual context-bound communicative acts. I suggest taking as paradigmatic not the creative metaphor but the literary work (conceived in aesthetic terms) and instead of concentrating on the kind of meaning involved in the Bible or liturgy I suggest concentrating on the special status of each and the modes of response peculiar to them.

Taking the literary work as paradigmatic in Warner's three topics—biblical interpretation, biblical translation and liturgical revision—is not meant to imply a conception of the Bible and liturgy as literature. That is an entirely separate enterprise and is hardly likely to advance the matter at issue, namely the attempt to explain some distinctively scriptural dimension. Rather, a parallel is being offered. Just as, so I believe, the aesthetic dimension of a literary work cannot be reduced to any particular feature of the meaning of its component sentences (explained in either semantic or pragmatic terms) so the scriptural dimension of a sacred text is not itself reducible to naturalized features of meaning.

Peter Lamarque

Perhaps the first attempt in modern critical theory to question the idea of meaning as a central concept of criticism comes in Cleanth Brooks' famous—one might say notorious—essay of 1947, 'The Heresy of Paraphrase' (Brooks 1968). There is much that is confused in that essay and its insights are often diffused by setting up too many targets, some of them straw men (the strict form/content distinction, the idea of poetry as statement, the critic as paraphraser, and so forth). But the core idea of a poem as a structural unity, an 'equilibrium of forces', as he puts it, became axiomatic in the development of New Critical thinking.

For our purposes what is of most interest is that this unity is explained not in linguistic or semantic terms but, albeit obscurely, as a unity of 'attitude'. And when Brooks elaborates on the kind of structure involved in poetry he draws on examples from the non-linguistic arts:

> The essential structure of a poem (as distinguished from the rational or logical structure of the 'statement' which we abstract from it) resembles that of architecture or painting: it is a pattern of resolved stresses. . . . The structure of a poem resembles that of a ballet or musical composition. It is a pattern of resolutions and balances and harmonizations, developed through a temporal scheme. (Brooks 1968: 166)

Brooks' central polemical point, of course, is that the content of a poem cannot be paraphrased into some independent statement on the basis of which the poem's truth, or even its value, might be judged. He could be understood merely as offering a holistic account of poetic meaning—the idea that the meaning of each component term or sentence is indivisible from the meaning of the whole—but he could also, and perhaps the points are not so far apart, be understood as shifting attention away from meaning altogether in the context of poetic criticism.

Unfortunately Brooks does not say enough to justify the special applicability of the heresy of paraphrase to poetry. Why should fine-grained connotation be an inseparable element of meaning in poetic language but not elsewhere? The poetic heresy of paraphrase calls for some further explanation. After all, it seems likely—as Warner himself has shown—that something comparable to the heresy of paraphrase applies also to the Bible and liturgy; but that does not entail reading either as poetry.

Why is it that the heresy of paraphrase seems to apply with particular force to writing of the kind found in poetry and sacred texts and the liturgy? The answer, I think, is not going to be found in trying to specify the kind of meaning possessed by these uses of language, be it in terms of a special illocutionary force or implicature or whatever. The trouble is the presence of those too, like the heresy of paraphrase, needs

118

explanation. Part of the answer must reside in the idea—already figured in Warner's account—that writing of this kind demands a distinctive mode of response, that special attention is drawn to internal relatedness (Brooks' 'structure'), that imaginative ability as well as knowledge of the language is necessarily invoked. If exactly the same content could be expressed in alternative ways then the internal structure of this way of saying it would be of only incidental importance.

Here Ted Cohen's notion of the 'cultivation of intimacy' is also helpful. Cohen asks about the purpose of metaphors and suggests that one important element is 'the capacity to form or acknowledge a . . . community and thereby establish an intimacy between the teller and the hearer' (Cohen 1979: 9). Although literal language can itself of course be used in the pursuit of intimacy there does seem to be a difference: 'In general, and with some obvious qualifications, it must be true that all literal use of language is accessible to all whose language it is. But a figurative use can be inaccessible to all but those who share information about one another's knowledge, beliefs, intentions, and attitudes.' (Cohen 1979: 7) Immediately this brings to mind again Augustine's *salubris obscuritas* and the idea that a positive benefit of biblical obscurity is to bind together the faithful, in the task of learning, and exclude the impious. It also recalls Wainwright's description of the liturgy, quoted by Warner (105), as 'a public act by which the worshippers identify themselves with a continuing community and enter into the "myth" of that community'.

Clearly the concepts of 'heresy of paraphrase' and 'cultivation of intimacy' are related, for part of what might be lost in paraphrase is precisely the intimacy of the original; the knowledge, beliefs, and attitudes elicited and presupposed by the poem or metaphor become dissipated when some literal rendering is offered in their place. Nevertheless, these two concepts, as applied to poetic and figurative usage, are still only signposts in the search for an understanding of the scriptural dimension of a sacred text.

What is needed also from the paradigm of the literary work is the idea of a 'literary institution', giving a focus and rationale for the mode of response definitive of literary appreciation (see Olsen 1978, 1987). It is only within the literary institution that the specific relevance of notions like 'heresy of paraphrase' and 'cultivation of intimacy'—not to speak of illocutionary force and imaginative demand—becomes apparent.

A work of literature is an 'institutional object', partly in the sense that there could be no works of literature independently of the institution that defines the concepts and conventions of literary appreciation, and partly in the sense that no formal characteristics, syntactic, semantic or more loosely 'rhetorical', can in themselves identify a text as literature. The point has implications for understanding literary works. Mere knowledge of a language is not sufficient to understand a piece of writing *as literature*. Although all the sentences, even the metaphors, in a poem might be understood by a reader, without knowledge of the institution the reader would have no conception of the point of the writing, what to make of it. 'Grasping the point', however, in this context, is not the same as recognizing the illocutionary intentions of the writer; that might be a necessary condition but it is not sufficient. The reader must also know the conventions of interpretation and evaluation constitutive of the practice of reading associated with the institution. This practice cannot be reduced to some independently characterised model of meaning or communication. The notions of illocutionary force, implicature, literal meaning, and so forth, could never provide an exhaustive description of the theoretical underpinnings of literary interpretation.

It is for these and other reasons that Stein Haugom Olsen, whose conception of literature I have summarised, suggests a shift of attention away from the concept of 'the meaning of a literary work' towards the idea of 'aesthetic' properties and a special mode of appreciation. Those who come to literature with theories of meaning, be they semiotic, semantic or communication-intention, get led into one form or another of reductionism. As Olsen puts it: 'The assumption that it is a *deep* truth about literature that a literary work is a verbal expression must be abandoned' (Olsen 1987: 66).

We seem to have come a long way from biblical interpretation and liturgical reform. But the paradigm of the literary institution—incorporating the insights of the 'heresy of paraphrase' and the 'cultivation of intimacy'—has much to commend it in this context. To understand what it might be to read the Bible *as Scripture*, as authoritative, to try to make sense of the notion of 'the Word incarnated in the word', it is clearly not enough to read the text as text and then somehow graft on the idea of Divine authorship. The conception of the text as authoritative Scripture must inform the reading process at every level, rather as the reading of a poem as a poem dictates the very nature of the attention given to it.

The mode of response appropriate to a scriptural reading is of course enormously difficult to characterise, but that it involves constraints of various kinds (not *any* reading can satisfy this description) and that it is distinctive from other modes of apprehension seem fairly clear. And these already suggest that the scriptural dimension can be illuminated by an institutional analysis, in the sense applied to literature. The idea of a practice, governed by norms and procedures recognized by a community of participants, is another important element in this conception. It also brings in the historical dimension. The norms of the practice have developed over time; 'cultivation of intimacy' is not only a relation between Scripture and individual readers but also between members of the historically based community. The shared insights, attitudes, experiences, background knowledge, and so forth, that bind this community together become epitomised in the institutional concepts and conventions.[1]

It would be wrong, however, to adopt either too mystical or too narrow a conception of the relevant community. There is no kind of Masonic mystery attached to members of the (historically extended) community who view the Bible as Scripture; nor should the 'institution' be identified too narrowly with some particular creed or denomination. The institution which defines the Bible as Scripture and thus dictates the mode of response appropriate to it is no different in principle from the institution which makes it possible for certain texts to be read as literature. The latter institution, along with the community of readers of literature, is not identified with a particular period or school of criticism (indeed it can accommodate a wide-ranging pluralism) nor is membership of the community imbued with mysterious privileges. Much the same is true of the institution that makes it possible to view the Bible as a sacred text.

Much more needs to be said, of course, about the concept of an institution applied to biblical interpretation. I hope I have said enough to make it look at least promising as a further location for Warner's insights drawn from the pragmatics of language, and in particular his emphasis on force, context-dependence and 'imaginative demand'. It should be clear, for example, how this conception could be brought to bear on the further problems of biblical translation and liturgical revision. The difficulties of translation connect in an obvious way to the heresy of paraphrase; the complex interrelatedness of style, structure and content make the very notion of 'saying the same thing' problematic. But the institutional analysis adds the further constraint on translation that the community of practitioners must have confidence not only that their same norms and procedures of reading remain applicable but also that they yield commensurate results in any adequate translation. It is not only the relation between text and translation, in some context-free sense, that is at issue, but the relation between text, translation and community. What, for example, the community of

---

[1] We might note also the way that dominant Christian metaphors are embedded in the norms and experiences of the community. Soskice makes this point: 'to explain what it means to Christians to say that God is a fountain of living water, or a vine-keeper, or a rock, or fortress, or king requires an account not merely of fountains, rocks, vines, and kings but of a whole tradition of experiences and of the literary tradition which records and interprets them.' (Soskice 1985: 158).

(competent) readers view as salient or significant from the scriptural point of view in an original rendering must not be lost or weakened in a translation.

Very similar points apply, obviously, to revision of the liturgy. The forms of worship reflect values as well as meanings and can help define the self-identity of the community. Paradigms or benchmarks, recognized as such by institutional norms, are bound to play a constraining role in reform. The old crux of 'ancient' versus 'modern' cannot be settled, or even competently debated, in terms independent of the institution which defines worship in the first place. In that sense the merits of revision can never be a purely secular issue, reducible to questions about implicature or aesthetics or poetry or contemporary morals or whatever.

One final caveat is in order. It is sometimes supposed that an appeal to institutions, in the technical sense advanced, involves an undesirable kind of compartmentalisation. So, it might be objected, if biblical interpretation is to be explained in institutional terms that will entail cutting the Bible off from other cognitive discourses. Once again, it might seem, at the very point where sense is being given to the concept of a scriptural dimension the import of this is weakened by relativising it within the bounds of a conventional—and of course human—practice.

But the objection is not well-founded. For one thing, the appeal to an institution—on the paradigm of the literary institution—was meant only to ground whatever special mode of apprehension might be involved in attending to the Bible as a sacred text; this was offered as an alternative grounding to that supplied by theories of meaning. As such it has no implications for either truth or reference. Theological realism, i.e. a commitment to the reality of God and the referential status of religious language (and metaphors), is quite compatible with taking an institutional view of the spiritual dimension of sacred texts. For what the latter implies is only that there are special forms of attention connected with reading a text as sacred, as authoritative, which belong in, and are defined by, a tradition. Those modes of response cannot be reduced to conceptions of meaning with their roots outside the institution. Here is Janet Martin Soskice with the final word:

> It is sometimes said that there is as much of Christian significance in the plays of Shakespeare as there is in the Old Testament; why not, therefore, regard the two equal as sources of revelation? Those who maintain this are greatly misled, not by irreverence for the sacred texts, but by insensitivity to the way texts are used within a literary tradition. In implying that revelation exists as a body of free-floating truths that can be picked up anywhere indifferently, they misunderstand the sense in which Christianity is 'a religion of the book'. (Soskice 1985: 154)

Religion and Ethics—I

STEWART SUTHERLAND

I

It was, I believe, Thomas Arnold who wrote: 'Educate men without religion and all you make of them is clever devils'. Thus the Headmaster of one famous school summarized pithily the view of the relationship between religion and ethics which informed educational theory and practice in this country for at least a further century. There is a confusion of two different assumptions usually to be found in this context. The first is that religious belief can provide an intellectual foundation (logical, or epistemological, or sometimes both) for moral belief; the second is that the effect of religious teaching is to improve behaviour according to the norms of some particular set of moral beliefs.

The second assumption offers too many hostages to fortune if it is construed as implying a one-to-one causal relationship, not to be vulnerable to a whole range of specific counter-examples. Thus there are examples of kind humanists and good atheists who clearly do not depend upon religious beliefs being either causes of, or reasons for, the goodness of their deeds. Equally there are all too many examples of evidence of the the activities of a worm at the moral core of piety, examples even of religious zeal giving rise to hatred or cruelty. It has been argued that in a less crudely individualistic fashion the social context of religious practice can provide nurture and support for good moral practice, but this is a rather vague notion unless it is refined significantly. I shall return to this point later.

On the former assumption that religious belief can provide some form of intellectual foundation for moral beliefs, the dilemma to which such an assertion has given rise has been classically and elegantly stated in Plato's *Euthyphro*: 'Is what is holy, holy because the gods approve it, or do they approve it because it is holy?' (Plato 1963: 10a) As, in the dialogue, Socrates interrogates the young Euthyphro, it becomes plain that Euthyphro holds together unreflectively a whole collection of beliefs about religion and morality, which upon analysis turn out to be incomplete. It is hardly the point of the dialogue to give a single answer to the question set above, or if so, then the dialogue fails. In so far as the dialogue is genuinely Socratic, then the point is to persuade Euthyphro of his (and our) ignorance, and by implication of the dangers of acting

Stewart Sutherland

(prosecuting his father) on the basis of unreflective and ill-formed beliefs.

However the form of the question set by Socrates to Euthyphro has given shape to much subsequent discussion: the issue is discussed by many, be they believer or unbeliever, philosopher or theologian, as an 'either . . . or'. *Either* what is good, is good because it is loved by God, or it is loved by God because it is good. Then the argument resolves itself into the question of whether the nature of goodness can be defined independently of reference to God, or the love of God.

To state my negative conclusion at the outset, I believe that this is an account of the nature of the relationship between religious belief and moral belief which is too simplistic, but to justify that conclusion and also the alternative account of the relationship I would propose, I must first outline some specific examples of cases where conflicts between religious and moral beliefs might arise.

II

A classic treatment of an example of the link between religious belief and moral beliefs is to be found in Kierkegaard's *Fear and Trembling*. Kierkegaard has his own agenda in that book, but the central problem around which all else is built is a series of discussions of the story of Abraham and Isaac. Kierkegaard defines the question posed by Abraham in a manner which is central to the concerns of this paper: 'The ethical expression for what Abraham did is, that he would murder Isaac; the religious expression is, that he would sacrifice Isaac.' (Kierkegaard 1954: 41) He specifies his aim in writing about Abraham thus:

> It is now my intention to draw out from the story of Abraham the dialectical consequences inherent in it, expressing them in the form of *problemata*, in order to see what a tremendous paradox faith is, a paradox which is capable of transforming a murder into a holy act well-pleasing to God.' (Kierkegaard 1954: 64)

Alongside this treatment of the theme it is instructive to consider Ibsen's *Brand*.[1] My contention is that in Brand, Ibsen is exploring the same issue. In fact, some parallels between Abraham and Brand are quite striking, and Geoffrey Hill who adapted *Brand* for the National Theatre company has underlined these parallels in his use of the words

[1] Ibsen, *Brand*; see particularly the version for the National Theatre by Geoffrey Hill (1978). I have discussed the relationship between Kierkegaard's account of Abraham, and Ibsen's account of Brand more fully in Sutherland 1980.

124

'dread', and 'trembling'. These, however, only serve to emphasize the parallels offered by Ibsen, who has Einar, a convert of Brand's, refer to God, who 'tested my poor worth / with sickness unto death'. (Ibsen 1978: Act V, p. 134) This is the same Einar who refers scoffingly to Brand as follows:

'You're good at breathing fire,
a real hot-gospeller;
that Fear-and-Trembling School,
has taught you very well!

(Act I, p. 11)

Yet more significant from my point of view are Brand's ruminations on what he takes to be a flaw in his wife's faith:

'Does she think God has qualms?—
the God who chose Abraham's
beloved child, the boy
Isaac, as the altar-stone
of his father's faith!'

(Act III, p. 62)

What Brand does not know is that it will come to this. Despite the warnings of the doctor that unless the family moves house Brand's young son will die, Brand believes it to be the will of God that they remain where they are. Thus Abraham's struggle over Isaac, passingly referred to by Brand, and which was Kierkegaard's preoccupation in *Fear and Trembling*, comes to be the story which Brand acts out in his own nineteenth century context.

Of course we come to classify Brand as mad; such single mindedness as he has shown, his impaling himself on the fork of 'all or nothing', his sacrifice successively of his mother's love, his child's life, and his wife's broken heart is itself insane. But what is the difference between Brand and Abraham, between insanity and faith? Kierkegaard implicitly assents to the validity of our question when he characterizes Abraham thus: 'Abraham was greater than all, great by reason of his power whose strength is impotence, great by reason of his wisdom whose secret is foolishness, *great by reason of his hope whose form is madness*, great by reason of the love which is hatred of oneself'. (Kierkegaard 1954: 31; my italics) The difference cannot be that Isaac was given a reprieve whereas Brand's child was not, for of course, as Kierkegaard stresses, Abraham could not know in advance of the outcome, if what he did is to be regarded as a definition of faith.

Kierkegaard has chosen his example well and, as he emphasizes, Abraham not only did keep silent, there was a sense in which he had to. However, Ibsen does open the window into Brand's deliberations. In

Abraham we see simply the deed done, the farewell to Sarah, the journey, the preparation of the altar. We know nothing of what goes on within. The story is a story of externals. Brand, however, occasionally bares his soul: he defends his actions, he worries over the lack of reconciliation with his mother, he briefly considers moving for the sake of his child's health. Indeed in the third Act we move with Brand to what he might call the final resolve of faith, to what others might regard as the final seduction by illness. The doctor has just persuaded Brand to quit his calling and move house for the sake of his son's health:

Doctor gazes silently at Brand who stands motionless looking in through the door; then he goes up to him, puts his hand on his shoulder, and says:

Doctor: For a man without remorse
              you're quick to compromise
              when the lamb to be slain
              is yours, your own first-born.
              One law for the world,
              another for your child,
              a double standard,
              is that it? You thundered
              'All or Nothing' in the ears
              of those poor villagers
              in their terror and want.
              You refused to forgive
              your mother unless she went
              naked to the grave.
              But now it's your turn
              to be the shipwrecked man
              clinging to the keel
              in the howling gale.
              What good are they now,
              those Tables of the Law?
              Your sermons on hell-fire,
              what a burden they are!
              Jettison them!
              Now it's sink or swim;
              and it's 'God keep him safe,
              my own darling boy!'
              You'd best be on your way.
              Take your child and your wife
              and go. And don't glance back
              at your forsaken flock.
              And don't spare a thought

for the hapless plight
of your mother's soul.
Renounce the Call.
Farewell, then, priest!
'Consummatum est'!

Brand clutches his head in bewilderment as if to collect his thoughts.

Brand: Have I been struck blind?
           Or was I blind before?

Doctor: Please don't misunderstand.
           I entirely applaud
           this change in your mood,
           I very much prefer
           the new family-man
           to the old Man-of-Iron.
           Believe me, I've spoken out
           for your own good. I've put
           a mirror in your hand.
           Look hard at what you find.
              Exit.

Brand: *(gazes for a while into space; suddenly he exclaims):*

           As I am now. . . as I was then. . .
           Where does truth end, error begin. . .?
           Blind man or seer, which man am I?
                                   (Act III, pp. 74–5)

Kierkegaard has warned us that this, or something like it, would happen. He has insisted that the move to unveil or reconstruct the inwardness of the man of faith will fail.

The issue which is explored in different ways by both Ibsen and Kierkegaard is logically related to the questions posed in Plato's *Euthyphro*. In the latter, in response to Euthyphro's stated intention of prosecuting his father, Socrates attempts to elicit from Euthyphro a clear understanding of what he is doing:

Socrates: But you, by heaven! Euthyphro, you think that you have
            such an accurate knowledge of things divine, and what is
            holy and unholy, that in circumstances such as you
            describe, you can accuse your father? You are not afraid
            that you yourself are doing an unholy deed?

Euthyphro: Why, Socrates, if I did not have an accurate knowledge of
            all that, I should be good for nothing, and Euthyphro
            would be no different from the general run of men.
                                   (Plato 1963: 4e–5a)

127

The issue quickly becomes the logical question of whether we define holiness in terms of what is loved by the Gods, or *vice-versa*. Euthyphro's unreflective self-confidence is found wanting.

There are one or two important points to be made about the examples from Kierkegaard and Ibsen to indicate the ways in which they advance the discussion. As a matter of fact both are concerned with the question of how, if at all, moral beliefs and sensitivities may modify a conviction based upon religious belief to act in ways contrary to moral intuitions. Of course, the examples could be re-cast to illustrate the converse. The central point which I wish to draw out, however, is that this clash of competing convictions occurs within the mind and soul of one individual. The dialogue quoted from *Brand* brings this out well, albeit eventually in Brand's own conception of what he is doing. The doctor confesses that he at best puts '. . . a mirror in your hand'. Whereas we see and hear something of Brand's to-ing and fro-ing as well as of his affirmation of resolution, with great subtlety Kierkegaard creates for us something of the inner turmoil of Abraham while at the same time making great play of the fact that throughout 'Abraham kept silent'. This latter point is of great significance for Kierkegaard, but Ibsen has counterpointed this by showing us what happens when the inner tension is given public expression within a social context. The initial point, however, is that the conflict is within the individual, quite as much as between individuals.

III

The second example which I wish to examine is that of euthanasia. Again a literary text can help. The title *Whose Life is it Anyway?* sets the question for us very well. The question is posed about Ken, completely paralysed from the neck down, after a road accident. The tension in the play is between Ken's wish to be discharged from hospital and thus detached from the various life-support mechanisms which keep him alive, and the professional duty accepted by his clinicians to keep him alive, even if that means detaining him against his (currently) stated will. The essence of Ken's case is not that he *wants* to die; nor, however, does he want to live at any price. There is the question of human dignity: '. . . but the dignity starts with . . . choice. If I choose to live, it would be appalling if society killed me. If I choose to die, it is equally appalling if society keeps me alive.' (Clark 1978: Act II, p. 78) The play is not directly concerned with a conflict between a religious and a secular ethic, although the hint of that is always there.

The consultant, Emerson, who tries to keep Ken in hospital against his will attempts to get the necessary second opinion to confirm his view that Ken's decision is not rational but is the reflection of a perfectly understandable state of depression. He asks a colleague to recommend a psychiatrist from, as the law requires, another hospital.

> *Dr Emerson*: [twinkling] And . . . do me a favour will you? Try and find an old codger like me, who believes in something better than suicide.
>
> *Dr Travers*: [grinning] There's a chap at Ellertree . . . a very staunch Catholic, I believe. Would that suit you?
>
> *Dr Emerson*: Be Jasus—sounds just the man!
> (Clark 1978: Act II, p. 49)

The reference there is to what is widely held to be what Thomas Wood calls 'the overwhelming weight of Christian opinion in the present as in the past':

> A human being is not the absolute owner of his or her life, whose creator and redeemer is God. One has the right to protect it but not the right wilfully to destroy it. Is it not a denial of God's loving providence to assert at any given time that one's life can no longer serve any good purpose? (Wood 1986: 211)

The difference between this example and the example of Brand (or possibly Abraham) is that whereas in the case of Brand the conflict in the end lies within the individual, in Brian Clark's play the conflict lies between individuals, and beyond that between different ways of formulating or giving ground to moral beliefs (as the following exchange between Ken and one of the other doctors illustrates):

> *Dr Scott*: But if you became happy?
>
> *Ken*: But I don't want to become happy by becoming the computer section of a complex machine. And morally you must accept my decision.
>
> *Dr Scott*: Not according to my morals.
>
> *Ken*: And why are yours better than mine?
> (Clark 1978: Act I, p. 39)

The differences between this case and the case of Brand/Abraham are two-fold. On the one hand the life at issue is Ken's own life, and on the other, the tension or disagreement lies between Ken and others. He is not subject to the vacillation and doubts of Brand. If he were, our reasonable reaction would be that he did not *really* want to die, and that therefore he must be prevented from following his 'chosen' course of action.

The moral and religious disagreements over the issue of abortion tend to fall into the even more complex area between the two examples, and the reasons for this have largely to do with the fact that if a play were written about abortion, rather than Ken's wish for voluntary euthanasia, the force of the question 'Whose life is it anyway?' would be very different indeed.

IV

In discussing the issues thrown into relief by these examples, I plan to proceed by drawing two distinctions which are fundamental. On the one hand it is important to distinguish between the following:

(a)(i)   In the context of Euthyphro's question and in its application to the examples given, there is in each case a knowable right answer to the problems posed; and

(a)(ii) The question posed by Abraham, Brand, and the dispute between Ken and his physician, in each case requires a decision which will have important consequences.

On the other hand, it is equally important to distinguish between the analytic truth:

(b)(i)   God always wills the good; and

(b)(ii) The God of Christian (or any other) theology always wills the good,

which if true is true synthetically.

My initial thesis is that in unreflective mode it is very easy to move from the urgency implied in (a)(ii) to the view made explicit in (a)(i). However there is no justification for arguing that because I may need to make a decision, there will be available to me the means of doing so, without error, if only I discover the path. I do not wish to commit myself in this paper to the extreme view that we can never *know* what is the right answer to a moral dilemma, for in one straightforward sense we can resolve some moral dilemmas by, for example, becoming aware of additional information. Thus whether to keep a new business engagement, or a promise to visit Great Aunt Agatha might be resolved by discovering on the one hand, that what I had thought to be a 'minor' engagement is one which will affect the livelihood of many employees, or on the other that Aunt Agatha is very ill. In either case I am not at all uncomfortable with the claim that we *know* what we ought to do.

However I do want to press the broader point that we may, and often do, find ourselves in dilemmas where a decision is required in advance of certainty. Indeed in most complex moral situations this is true. This does not absolve us from deciding and acting; it is rather one mark of what it means to talk of the limits of finitude. It is also characteristically a mark of those dilemmas which seem to, or indeed do, involve a clash between religious and moral premises. This is true whether it is a question of the inner shifts between certainty and uncertainty in Brand's struggles, or of the differing perspectives and responsibilities which pull Ken and Emerson in opposite directions.

In an ideal, or a-historical, world it may well be that there is a correlation to be established between the existence of questions and the availability of correct answers, which we can *know* to be correct, but in the world of space and time which we inhabit there is no one-to-one correlation; in practice the decisions often cannot wait upon answers which at best are there 'in principle'. It is only in an unreflective state that we could consider the situation to be otherwise.

Of course, there are both reflective and unreflective concerns which arise from the clear statement of such a view. At one end of the spectrum, these fears take the form of a question:

Q(i) Are there then no absolute truths in this context?

At the other, the question becomes more philosophically sophisticated:

Q(ii) Are you then espousing a form of subjectivism based on the premise that there are certain religious/moral dilemmas to which there are no objective solutions?

In the final section of this paper I shall give my response to these questions, by simultaneously outlining an approach to the *'Euthyphro'* dilemma which suggests that it is misconceived.

V

The question posed in the *'Euthyphro'* dilemma has the application to Brand, that if he were to settle first the question of whether moral belief or religious belief is to be given the logical priority, then he could draw inferences about the correct course of action. The implication for Abraham, according to Kierkegaard, is that he has chosen to follow the call of religious rather than moral duty. Conversely Ibsen urges us through his characterization of Brand to give the priority to the family concerns of care for the health of the children rather than the vocational call to minister to the flock on the north side of the mountain. The clash it seems is clear; if one could only solve the *'Euthyphro'* dilemma then the correct decision would follow. My contention is that the search for an answer which has the character of an absolute, driven by the implications of finality in the decision which is to be taken, is misconceived.

As I have suggested above, it is important to distinguish between the two different propositions:

(b)(i) God always wills the good;

and

(b)(ii) The God of Christian (or any other) theology always wills the
good.

The second proposition is synthetic. As such it is not involved in the
questions raised by Socrates' cross-examination of Euthyphro, for it
makes a claim about particular systems of religious belief and the
picture of God embodied in them, rather than about God *per se*. To
raise a question about the latter would only be possible if we regarded
ourselves as having a clear picture of what God wills (as distinct from
what the Church, or a guru, or a particular book tells us that He wills)
and found *that* in opposition to our moral beliefs or intuitions. My
central question concerns how we could possibly come to have such a
clear view of the will of God, apparently arrived at without reference to
our moral sensibilities. My recommendation, or indeed prescription, is
to avoid that state by concentrating our discussion on the second,
synthetic, proposition about the God of Christian or any other
theology.

This however leaves unanswered the legitimate question of the truth
of the first proposition—(b)(i) 'God always wills the good'. The manner of the truth of this proposition is related to its status. My proposal is
that it should be accorded the status of an analytic truth, and that as
such the tests of the truth of (b)(i) are those appropriate to analytic
truths. The implication of this is that whereas (b)(ii) may be open to
falsification in principle, for it is at least in part empirically based, this is
not so in the case of (b)(i). Despite this, however, I do not wish to
suggest that (b)(i) is unimportant, or of 'merely' linguistic significance.
The rôle of (b)(i) is to assert a fundamental belief about the ultimate
compatibility and indeed interdependence of moral and religious
beliefs. It is a neat formula whose analytic status reflects the primary
significance which it has in the system of ideas which this paper is
intended to define. It is also, however, a potentially very misleading
formula, for it seems to be asserting a straightforwardly descriptive
truth about the goodness of a being called God. This picture misleads
us with regard to both the content and the status of (b)(i).

This, of course, gives an entirely different character to the dilemma
posed by the *Euthyphro*. The search by Brand and Abraham for the
right decision, the right action, is no longer a dispute between the
priority of the moral or the priority of the religious, understood in
absolute and antithetical terms. The search is now for an understanding
of the options which face either Brand or Abraham in the light of the
claim that the decision made should reflect the will of a God who

(analytically) wills the good. It is no longer a question whether God wills what is good; the question is whether this interpretation of the will of God is actually an interpretation of the will of God, rather than a misinterpretation of the will of God.

The gain in both realism and understanding is very great. Now there need be no puzzle about using moral criteria to evaluate religious claims, nor indeed the converse. This, I suggest, illustrates the reality observed in many religions. Thus, for example, in the Old Testament the prophets regularly appeal to moral criteria to evaluate religious claims. So St Paul reminds us in I Corinthians xiii that in the absence of love the greatest of religious gifts are of little value and there is no doubt that the gifts include those of proclamation and teaching. Equally the idea of *jihad* in Islam is not only over-simplified in most references to it in the non-Islamic press, but is itself in application to specific situations subject to evaluation by criteria which are evidently moral. Thus, within Islam there is a strong prohibition against waging wars for the sake of acquiring worldly glory or power. This is not best understood as moral opposition to the religious idea of *jihad*, but rather as part of the discussion of whether this action (which if it is the will of Allah is good) is the will of God.

The converse situation is also envisaged in the account which I am giving. Thus what someone might regard as a moral absolute might be modified as a result of growth of religious insight or by a process of reflection on religious teaching. For example, it is quite conceivable that someone who regarded the embryo or the foetus as, in principle, (pre-birth) no different from any other discardable piece of tissue from the human body, might change that view if for quite other reasons he or she came to an understanding of creaturehood incompatible with this. Alternatively, someone might move from the view that some wars are justified, to a position of pacifism *via* the same route. On the view which I am elaborating, this would include a change of moral perception, or change in the understanding of what moral goodness is. It would not be the defeat of moral criteria by religious criteria.

The fundamental point is that the traditional way of setting the question posed by the *Euthyphro* presumes that we have clear knowledge of what the will of God is, quite independently of our moral perception. This, I believe, is a misunderstanding of the analytic connection which I am proposing between 'the will of God' and 'what is good'. When it comes to knowing what the will of God is, or even what is good, we cannot have such analytically based certainty. We have, at best, fitful attempts by human beings, including philosophers and theologians, to understand how to apply such terms in our finite world of time and space.

The point of the assertion of the analytic connection between the 'will of God' and 'what is good' is to underline the claim that to take such a view of human reflection on morality and religion is not inevitably to be committed to either a subjectivist or relativist account of this.

Religion and Ethics—II

A. PHILLIPS GRIFFITHS

Professor Sutherland has argued that 'God wills the good' should be regarded as an analytic truth, with the consequence that any account of what is God's will in which it does not appear to be good is either a mistake about God's will or a mistake about what is good.

To respond with a quibble: to hold that 'God wills the good' is analytic would seem to give rise to a new ontological argument, thus:

> If it is analytically true that God wills the good, then necessarily God wills the good;
> It is necessarily true that anything which wills must exist;
> Therefore necessarily God exists.

Some such difficulty may arise from treating any proposition the subject term of which is a name or a uniquely referring expression as analytic. However, Sutherland's purpose might be served if we treat the analytic relation he wants as one between predicates, which might be expressed by 'If something is the will of God, then it is good'. That is much the same as to say that the relation is between concepts, which need not be instantiated in any existent thing or things. If so, such a relation cannot depend on how any existent thing or things actually are. This immediately gives rise to the question: on what, then, could any such relation depend? How can the assertion of such a relation be justified?

One obvious way is if the relation between the concepts is one of identity, as in 'eggs are eggs'. It is obvious that the proposition 'God wills the good' is not meant to imply such a relation, such that 'God' is then to mean no more than 'whatever wills the good'. For this proposition to be edifying there must be some other predicates which apply to God; that is to say, God must be conceived as a being which has some characteristics over and above that of willing the good.

As Kant says, every analysis requires a previous synthesis; that is to say, the elements of the description, the characteristics regarded as inseparably contained in the concept, need to be held together. Clearly any set of mutually compatible characteristics can be thought of as held together. But a synthesis may be arbitrary, idle and pointless: for example, if someone were to define a concept 'cabwaxpinkstrinking' as a cabbage tied with pink string sealed by wax owned by a king. Or, while not involving any contradiction, it may be the concept of something which is not in any serious sense possible. Thus for example, the proposition 'A ship's clock tells accurate time at sea' may simply be a definition of the term 'ship's clock' but, Kant says, the term 'ship's clock' can hardly be said even to represent a concept, unless we know how it is possible to put together a clock which tells accurate time at sea, which he mistakenly thought in 1781 nobody did.

Sutherland says that he does not wish to suggest that 'God wills the good' is trivial; rather it asserts 'a fundamental belief about the ultimate compatibility and indeed interdependence of moral and religious beliefs'. The term 'ultimately' is clearly of the first importance here. Indeed some qualification is obviously essential, for religious beliefs (those of Buddhists, Christians and Aztecs) are not compatible with *each other*, let alone with our moral beliefs; any more than are the moral beliefs of libertarians and Mrs Whitehouse. It cannot be, as Sutherland points out, that the analytic truth 'God wills the good' is true of *whatever* is regarded as God's will in every actual theological position; nor, unless I am unspeakably arrogant, could it mean that *whatever* I may believe to be morally good, constitutes God's will. How then are we to understand this belief that this compatibility and interdependence of our moral and religious beliefs is, if not actual, nevertheless ultimate? It seems to me that this belief can only be that if we reflected long and hard and well enough—and that might always be better than we will ever be capable of reflecting—our religious and moral beliefs would then be compatible and interdependent.

But how could anyone have such a belief, unless they believed that such reflection leads us nearer to the truth; and that the truth is: that what really is the case regarding God's will is compatible with what really is morally good? That not only, as Sutherland says, 'such a view of human reflection on morality and religion is not inevitably to be committed to either a subjectivist or relativist account of this', but that it is strictly contrary to any such anti-realist position?

The difficulty now appears that the grounding on which one can justify treating 'God wills the good' as analytic depends on our belief that it is true that God wills the good; though *this* belief is not in an analytic proposition—it is that there is *in fact* God who *in fact* wills what is *in fact* the good.

Another difficulty is that the thesis depends on our being able to discriminate—not necessarily in any systematic way, not through the setting out of formal necessary and sufficient conditions, but broadly, or at any rate so that we can be confident of some clear cases—religious from other beliefs, and moral from other beliefs.

When someone—in this case, admittedly, a madman—is represented as saying 'As flies to wanton boys, are we to the gods; They kill us for their sport' (*King Lear* IV.i.36–7), can we treat him as expressing a religious belief? The question is not, whether what he believes is true. We might say 'Yes, that's true; but the gods are not God'.

But what if such a man believes much the same, but that there is only one god, whom he calls 'God'? Who is, he says, the one maker and sustainer of all things, and that the way God treats people—like boys treat flies—is morally outrageous. He accepts some of the propositions about God which we too accept as analytic. But one may still be very reluctant to say that his is a religious belief; any more than is Schopenhauer's doctrine of the Will, or the belief of a Lucretian materialist that all is atoms and the void, which are no respecters of persons. These are not religious beliefs, perhaps not even irreligious beliefs: but rather beliefs which leave no room for a religious attitude.

So perhaps we can characterize religious beliefs as those which are inherent in a religious attitude, allowing that different religious attitudes may accommodate different beliefs. In the same way, we might characterize moral beliefs as those which are inherent in a moral attitude, allowing that different moral attitudes may accommodate different beliefs. Furthermore, the expression of a given belief may or may not be the expression of a religious belief: e.g. 'There is one maker and sustainer of all things'; similarly, 'Do not be one of those forever tippling wine nor one of those who gorge themselves with meat' may be a moral injunction, or only a counsel of prudence when the reason given for it is 'for the drunkard and glutton impoverish themselves, and a drowsy head makes a wearer of rags'. (Proverbs xxiii 20–21)

The grip, the phenomenological ineluctability, if not the analyticity, of the conviction that God wills the good would be explained if the moral attitude is inherent in, and cannot but inform, the religious attitude.

The religious attitude is the attitude of worship (and thus the mad Gloucester's cry cannot be regarded as religious). God is the proper object of worship, and we call idolatry the misdirection of that attitude to the 'gods' or the many baals. These are not worthy of praise as holy (the question of their existence is relatively minor).

So the psalmist begins 'Shout for joy to Yahweh, all virtuous men, praise comes well from upright hearts . . .'; and then himself gives praise: '. . . he loves virtue and justice, Yahweh's love fills the earth' (Psalm xxxiii). That surely *is* praise: and a denial of it would seem to be blasphemy.

So also St Anselm gives praise in *Proslogion II*, addressing God as One than which no greater can be conceived. As critics of Anselm's ontological argument say, he already presupposes the truth of his conclusion. But this criticism already hints at an apology. As the late Norman Malcolm in his admittedly very flawed defence of Anselm (1960) puts it, 'this language-game is played'; having in mind of course

A. Phillips Griffiths

Wittgenstein's notion of a language-game as a way of living: not a mere contrived word-ritual, but a genuine ritual, like, as Wittgenstein (1980: 8e) puts it, a kiss. To one for whom praise of God is part of the way he lives, the existence of God is not so much analytic as beyond question, in the way that no historian questions the existence of the universe in the past. A boy learning to do history might be encouraged by the teacher if he raised the question whether Richard III really did murder the princes in the Tower; but if he insisted on questioning whether the past is real, he would, as Wittgenstein says (1969: paras 310–317), be asked to leave the class. For this reason, for anyone for whom holy praise is part of the way he lives not only is God's existence unquestioned; that God is good is for him, whether or not analytic, beyond question.

It seems to me that the latter demand, that God's goodness is beyond question, is even greater than the demand that He exists. It may be one which leads to atheism, a religious atheism: someone might find that to praise, laud and magnify His holy name demanded that He could not be within or beside this sorry scheme of things—a kind of demythologized Manicheism. It is an attitude which has been held, though so far as I know not by anyone of theological distinction.

In saying all this I am not disagreeing with Sutherland's conclusion; I am merely giving my own reasons for agreeing with it. But there is a difficulty I think we must both face, one raised in considering Kierkegaard (1939) in his meditation on Abraham. Our topic is ethics and religion. In praising God as good, must we conceive goodness in any ethical sense? May it not be that ethical goodness is not a particular kind of goodness appropriate to Holy praise?

When I was a small boy I was not allowed to read a book at table, so I had to make do with reading the top of the Marmite pot. There I read that the crystals in Marmite were not to be feared, since they were an essential part of its goodness. But even in those far off-days, knowing that God is good, I did not imagine that he must contain Marmite crystals. At the same time I didn't doubt that the crystals were an essential part of the special kind of goodness I was happy to believe Marmite to have, so much liking the taste. In the same way someone may not rate ethical goodness as an essential part of the special kind of goodness God has, without doubting it to be a special kind of goodness.

This difficulty is exacerbated by the fact that the notion of morality is temporally local. The attitudes of primitive, or at least radically alien, people to practices such as cutting off the foreskin or the clitoris, eating black pudding and having blood transfusions may have some practical similarities to moral attitudes, but no more. Perhaps with regard to such people it may not be possible to identify anything which is clearly, rather than merely analogically, a moral attitude. On the other hand it may be possible, though with some difficulty, to attribute religious attitudes to them. Obviously, in such cases moral attitudes could not be regarded as informing the religious attitude. On the other hand, their religious attitudes could not be criticized as incompatible with a moral attitude they do not have; though they may be incompatible with our moral attitudes.

This fact then cannot bear against such an inherence for those who do have moral attitudes. It is surely very difficult for the ordinary decent middle class person to accuse God of being immoral, laying so much store by morality and regarding it as an immensely important good; and no doubt being as impatient with this suggestion as with ethical scepticism which he treats as mere philosophical prattle. What I shall now argue is that such decent people cannot easily be robbed of their convictions, if they are sufficiently tough-minded. For such a person it is difficult to see what could count, not as a counter-example, but *finding* a counter-example, to them. And I shall argue that Kierkegaard's counter-example, Abraham's taking God's will as contrary to the morality of fatherhood, is not only not convincing as a particular case but a consequence of his mistaken notion of ordinary morality.

For Kierkegaard Abraham faces three different imperatives: one arising from his natural love of his son, one arising from universal ethics, and one that is the command of God. The first two are in conflict with the third; but, Kierkegaard insists, it is the conflict between the ethical and the religious which is important. The first conflict is he says a mere tribulation. It is the second which makes Abraham a knight of faith. If we take this case seriously, then not taking it seriously we must first ask what was the morality of this man which was in conflict with God's imperative. All we have to hand to achieve this are the recorded doings of his life (Genesis xii–xxv).

Abram, as he then was, came up from Chaldea (oddly enough the place where the chosen people came from who took over Judea after the second exile a thousand years later) because he believed God had spoken to him, promising to dispossess the benighted inhabitants of Canaan in his favour. However, things did not go well at first because of a famine in Canaan; so Abram went to Egypt, where he concealed the fact that he was married to his half-sister (Genesis xii 10–13 & xx 12; being unaware of Leviticus xx 17, he did not offer himself for public execution). Pharaoh innocently took her into his house, and showered Abram with gifts of animals and people for his sister's sake. But God was angry with Pharaoh for taking another man's wife, and gave him the plague. Pharaoh discovered the reason and said to Abram 'What is this you have done to me?' (Genesis xii 18) He then told Abram to leave Egypt with his sister, though allowing him to keep all the gifts. Later,

A. Phillips Griffiths

Abram, now Abraham, went to the Philistines, where he did exactly the same thing to the King, Abimelech, who said to him 'What have you done to us?'. (xx 9) However, he did not send Abraham away: he showered him with gifts and land. Abraham afterwards bitterly reproved Abimelech for allowing one of his servants to seize one of Abraham's wells.[1]

Abraham also believed he had heard God tell him to cut the foreskins off all the males he owned over eight days old (xvii 9–14). (This would immediately show him to be a Kierkegaardian knight of faith, if like a decent middle class Englishman he would surely have regarded child abuse as a moral outrage.) He next believed he heard God tell him to kill not only his eldest son, but his wife's slave, the boy's mother, as well (xxi 12). The boy, previously a boy of fifteen (in the *Yahwist* version; xvi 16, xxi 5, 8—see also xvii 25), was now again a babe in arms (in the *Elohist* version; xxi 14) who had mocked Abraham's wife (xxi 9; *Authorised Version*). Abraham was told to send them out into the desert with a small amount of water, which as far as he knew should have meant certain death: again a knight of faith's defiance of morality. But just as Hagar, Ishmael's mother, was about to die of thirst God opened her eyes to a well, and they survived (xxi 15–20). Now it could be said that this is unfair to Abraham: he believed that in the same breath God had told him that Ishmael would father a nation (xxi 13); so obviously God would not let Ishmael die, whatever might have happened to his poor mother. The same can be said in defence of Abraham's behaviour to his younger son, Isaac. A priest told me the other day that this was one of the most immoral acts ever recorded; but Abraham believed God had told him that Isaac would also father a nation. At any rate, it seems to me that what goes for the one case goes for the other.

My account, accurate to the point of fundamentalist asininity, is truer than Kierkegaard's fantasy, which seems to me to be reminiscent of the worst kind of sentimental Victorian church stained glass window.

But my account is asinine because, tongue-in-cheek, it makes Abraham out to be a very wicked man, or at least an evil paranoiac like the Yorkshire Ripper who heard voices, telling him to kill women, coming out of tombstones. Or, perhaps, as having quite extraordinary moral attitudes. Whereas it is extremely difficult to attribute to Abraham any

---

[1] It is interesting enough for me to diverge here to remark that Abraham's son Isaac later did exactly the same thing to Abimelech. It was God who told Abimelech about Abraham's Sarah, but he found out about Isaac when he looked out of his window and saw the old man frisking with Rebekah. What Abimelech now said was 'What is this you have done to us?' (Genesis xxvi 10). But he didn't send him away. He protected Isaac who got very rich, though Isaac also, to stretch the coincidence beyond belief, had trouble with the Philistines over his wells.

moral attitudes at all. Obviously completely uncivilized, Abraham seems to predate not only horticulture and urbanity but morality: a man of the *jahaliyya*, without the law.

How far, indeed, should we credit Abraham with religious attitudes, taking the bare narrative as it is, without the benefit of hindsight; remembering, indeed, that the narrative itself is written a thousand years later—with the benefit of hindsight, rather like the contemporary liberal's interpretation of the story of Magna Carta?

I have no idea how people who lived nomad lives and had concubines and slaves thought of the institution of fatherhood; whether sons were thought of as potential allies, or property, or guarantors of the only kind of immortality it was supposed there can be, that of one's seed. Did itinerant sheiks like Abraham change their offspring's napkins, dandle them on their knees, or even know them as well as the average headmaster knows his pupils? Or love them better than a headmaster loves his star scholarship pupil?

Why is God said to have told Abraham to make a holocaust of his son in Moriah, a high place, a journey days away (xxi 1–4)? There is speculation that the celebrant of a sacrifice thereby laid claim to the place where it was made. Has this got something to do with some now forgotten territorial dispute?

I do not know whether the significance of the altercations about wells were simply about the ownership of water—of course important enough in itself—or whether wells were generally regarded as holy places, like Beersheba with its tamarisk (xxi 33): a miraculous springing of water from the dry land showing God's favour and bounty, so that it would matter very much to whom it was directed.

And since the contents of Chapter xvii of Genesis concerning circumcision are supposed to be a priestly interpolation made after the Second Exile, it is daft to speculate what light this throws on the moral attitudes of Abraham.

So can an example of a real conflict between morality and religion disturbing to the decent Christian be found analogous to that of the Abraham of Kierkegaard's fantasy?

It is extraordinarily difficult for me to do so. I may of course lack literary imagination, or knowledge of that of others. I do not think Ibsen's *Brand* will do: certainly it wasn't meant to. Graham Greene's *The Heart of the Matter* comes to mind: but the conflict there is with love of God and love of a person, not explicitly religion and morality. It is not a very plausible one, according to Monsignor Alfred Gilbey. 'I mean, the book was quite ridiculous' he says; 'When it comes to God and a mistress, there's simply no choice, is there?' (Mortimer 1991). It reminds one of St Augustine's rejection of his common law wife and son; but there again, at best one can only say *autres temps, autres mœurs*.

I am not dogmatically saying that there could not be a case of this conflict. I am reminded of the medieval puzzles, motivated more by an interest in logic than any serious religious conflict, about what to say if God should command one to disobey him. How can I rule out that I should hear that command, and not know how to obey it without disobeying it or disobey it without obeying it, and it yet should truly be God's command? How can I know that there is something God may not do, unless asserting it is a contradiction; and it is not a contradiction to assert that someone gives a contradictory command. But since I know that the influence of black bile, or sheer base motivation, has very often led people to hear things that were not in fact said, and since I cannot conceive what would be the significance of such a temptation, isn't it reasonable for me to reject it as truly coming from God? Indeed, might not God truly be tempting me by a paradox: tempting me to take as His command what is in fact His command but one which my love and reverence for Him should lead me to say it is not?

What I am saying is that I am unable to conceive of any circumstances in which someone, whether myself or another, can be judged to have been commanded by God to do something wrong, evil, or wicked. That it is such surely at least casts immense doubt; and explanations in terms of black bile are known to be true, whereas there is none except perhaps the mythical case of Abraham where the opposite is generally taken to be true. One cannot take such doubts lightly. The general verdict would be that the case is one of someone either mad or bad; but that is only because it is the general verdict that all supposed divine inspiration is just madness, or superstition. However, if someone were convinced that he had direct divine inspiration impelling him to go and preach to the Godless Coventrians, the Church would not necessarily think him mad: this might very well be a movement of the Holy Spirit. But on the other hand, not necessarily; he might be a really potty fellow, who would be better occupied teaching philosophy. It would be a question, to be properly gone into, as to which. But the mundane explanation would surely be overwhelmingly more plausible in the case of a man who told his parish priest that God had told him to kill his beloved grandmother.

In speaking of the difficulty of plausibly specifying a case of finding an example of this radical conflict I have assumed no more than that God is the object of our worship and holy praise, and that we have ordinary decent moral attitudes. The difficulty becomes greater still if we hold certain views of the nature of the moral, for example those of St Thomas Aquinas or Bishop Butler. But there is one view of the moral in terms of which the conflict, even if we can give no plausible living example of it, becomes inevitable. It is, I think, one generated by Kant, and one which seems to be adopted by Kierkegaard *via* Hegel.

> In Hegelian philosophy *das Äussere* (*die Entäusserung*) [the outer] is superior to *das Innere* [the inner]. This is often explained by an example. The child is *das Innere* the man *das Äussere*; and it follows that the child is determined by the external while the man as *das Äussere* is determined by *das Innere*. On the other hand, faith is this paradox, that inwardness is superior to the external. . . .
>
> For the ethical conception of life, then, the Individual lies under an obligation to purge himself of his inwardness and to express it in an external. Every time he shrinks from it, every time he limits himself to a sentiment or disposition which belongs to inwardness or slips back into it again, he sins against himself and lies under tribulation. The paradox of faith is that there is an inwardness incommensurable in terms of the external, an inwardness which, it is important to note, is in no way identical with the former, but is a new inwardness. This must not be overlooked. The new philosophy has merely allowed itself to substitute 'the immediate' for 'faith'. But it is absurd to do this and at the same time to deny that faith has existed in all ages, and in this way faith joins the rather vulgar company of sentiments, sensations, idiosyncrasies, vapours, etc. (Kierkegaard 1939: 98–99)

The essence of Kierkegaard's notion of morality is epitomized here. '. . . in duty itself I enter into no relation to God' he has said (1939: 97): the ethical is the universal, understood in an entirely abstract sense; so, he says, 'It rests immanent in itself, having nothing outside itself which is its *telos*' (1939: 75).

He thus echoes Kant's view that the moral will is the will that wills itself, and is determined by no object. It is an autonomous will, as opposed to a heteronomous will which is directed to some object. Empirical heteronomy consists in a will directed to some empirical object; to be distinguished from rational heteronomy, which is directed to some rational object, such as perfection. To act morally is to act from the conception of abstract rational law as such, whereas all other action is determined by the conception of a particular state of affairs, whether it is empirical or rational heteronomy. So also for Kierkegaard: faith is a passion, it is more like sentiment or sensation or idiosyncrasy, in which a particular individual is related to a particular object; and it is distinguished from other passions and sentiments only in that its object is what (following Hegel) Kierkegaard calls God, the Absolute.

The objection which this conception of morality runs—and ran—into immediately is Hegel's: that it would appear impossible that morality should have any content, having nothing to appeal to but

A. Phillips Griffiths

contentless abstract rationality as such, or the notion of pure law. Kant does try to show that edifying moral judgments such as 'one ought not to make lying promises' or 'one ought to foster one's talents' can nevertheless arise from this, 'as from their principle', but his arguments are very bad ones. However, both he and Kierkegaard do hold that one ought to love one's neighbour. Kant initially deduces only that one should help others in need, but as we shall see he does connect this with the Dominical injunction. Kant writes:

> The dependence of a contingently determinable will on principles of reason is called an *interest*. Hence an interest is found only where there is a dependent will which in itself is not always in accord with reason: to a divine will we cannot ascribe any interest. But even the human will can *take an interest* in something without therefore *acting from interest*. The first expression signifies *practical* interest in the action; the second *pathological* interest in the object of the action. The first indicates only dependence of the will on principles of reason by itself; the second its dependence on principles of reason at the service of inclination. . . . (Kant 1948: 81n.)

Now one can immediately see why this should give rise to an apparent contradiction between morality—reverence for abstract rational law as such—and religion. For the religious man, the man of faith, does not merely take an interest in God, he acts from an interest in God: to love God is at least not to want to offend *Him*, and not merely for fear of His wrath; and to act on this is to act from this very interest, not from a reverence for law as such. Thus for example Scobie, in Graham Greene's *The Heart of the Matter*, conceives himself in sinning as adding to the suffering of Christ on the cross. Consider also:

> Thou wilt be sick with love, and yearn for Him,
> And feel as though thou coulds't but pity Him,
> That one so sweet should e'er have placed Himself
> At disadvantage such, as to be used
> So vilely by a being so vile as thee.
> There is a pleading in His pensive eyes
> Will pierce thee to the quick, and trouble thee.[2]

The Divine will to which Kant refers, having no interest in anything, and hence not in the creation, is not God at all. Kierkegaard sees this, or at any rate something confusedly like it, when he writes:

> The ethical is the universal, and as such it is also the divine. It is therefore true to say that all duty is fundamentally towards God; but

[2] John Henry Newman, *The Dream of Gerontius*, quoted in Strange: 1990. I am grateful to Fr Martin Jarrett-Kerr, CR for drawing my attention to this article.

if one cannot add anything to this, it is the same as saying that I have no real duty towards God. Duty becomes duty when it is related to God, but in duty itself I enter into no relation with God. It is thus duty to love one's neighbour. It is duty in that it is related to God, but in duty I enter into no relation with God, but into a relation with the neighbour I love. And, if in this connexion, I say that it is my duty to love God, I am simply announcing a tautology, in so far as God, in this case, is understood in an altogether abstract sense as the divine, i.e. the universal, i.e. duty. . . . God becomes an invisible vanishing point, a thought without power. (Kierkegaard 1939: 97)

But this does not really represent any conflict between religion and ethics: it represents only a conflict between religion and a quite wrong-headed notion of ethics.

What Kierkegaard does not notice, in the passage just quoted, is that in precisely the same way and for precisely the same reasons, in duty so conceived I do not enter into any relationship, of the required sort, with my neighbour either. I do not do what Jesus said I should do, love my neighbour (Mark xii 31): I act to all external appearance as if I loved my neighbour. My duty is to the moral law, not to my neighbour. Thus Kant on this specific point:

It is doubtless in this sense that we should understand too the passages from Scripture in which we are commanded to love our neighbour and even our enemy. For love out of inclination cannot be commanded; but kindness done from duty—although no inclination impels us, and even though natural and unconquerable disinclination stands in our way—is *practical*, and not *pathological*, love, residing in the will and not in the propension of feeling, in principles of action and not of melting compassion. (Kant 1948: 67)[3]

Now I believe Jesus meant what He said, not what Kant thinks: He meant that we should learn compassion, not just to act compassionately. Consider the corporal work of mercy (Matthew xxv 31–46). The heavenly King says to those who are saved 'I was hungry and you gave me food'. The virtuous ask 'Lord, when did we see you hungry?'. The King answers 'So far as you did this to the least of these brothers of

---

[3] It is a corollary of this doctrine for Kant that all non-moral motivation is essentially selfish; for the agent aims only at the satisfaction of (which Kant mistakenly thinks is the same as the satisfaction to be gained from) *his* inclination towards the particular object. Kierkegaard seems also to share this error. He says 'Then why did Abraham do this? For God's sake, and so, what is absolutely identical, for his own sake. For God's sake, because God demands a proof of his faith; for his own sake, because he wanted to furnish this proof' (1939: 84). See Griffiths 1991.

mine, you did it to me'. Now the virtuous did not know, when they fed the hungry, that they were also feeding the King—at least, not those in the parable, though we know it now. Which puts us in some difficulty. We may have to say to the King 'Lord, I fed the hungry: not of course because I cared a monkey's toss for them: if I hadn't been aware that in doing so I was doing it to you, I'd have kicked them from the door'. Would we then be judged to be among the virtuous? And would we be among the virtuous if we did it for Kant's republican substitute for the King, the abstract form of law?

References

Anscombe, G. E. M. and Geach, P. T. 1961. *Three Philosophers: Aristotle, Aquinas, Frege*. Oxford: Blackwell.

Anselm 1940–68. *Anselmi Opera Omnia*, ed. F. S. Schmitt, 6 vols. Rome and Edinburgh: Nelson.

Anselm 1962. *Saint Anselm: Basic Writings*, trans. S. N. Deane, 2nd edn. La Salle, Illinois: Open Court.

Augustine 1947. *Christian Instruction (De doctrina Christiana)*, trans. J. J. Gavigan, in L. Schopp and R. J. Defarri (eds), *The Fathers of the Church: Writings of Saint Augustine*, vol. 4. Washington, DC: Catholic University of America Press.

Augustine 1961. *Confessions*, trans. R. S. Pine-Coffin. Harmondsworth: Penguin.

Augustine 1963. *The Confessions of St. Augustine*, trans. R. Warner. New York: Mentor Books.

Austin, J. L. 1962. *How to Do Things With Words*. Oxford: Clarendon Press.

Ayer, A. J. 1936. *Language, Truth and Logic*. London: Gollancz.

Bambrough, J. R. 1969. *Reason, Truth and God*. London: Methuen.

Bambrough, J. R. 1979. *Moral Scepticism and Moral Knowledge*. London: Routledge.

Barrett, D. C. 1991. *Wittgenstein on Ethics and Religious Belief*. Oxford: Blackwell.

Barth, K. 1932–70. *Die kirchliche Dogmatik*, 4 vols., 13 parts. Chr. Kaiser and EVZ-Verlag: Munich and Zurich.

Bell, M. 1988. *F. R. Leavis*. London and New York: Routledge.

Bochenski, I. M. 1948. 'On Analogy', *The Thomist* xi, 424–447.

Brooks, C. 1968. *The Well-Wrought Urn*. London: Dobson.

Burnet, J. 1930. *Early Greek Philosophy*, 4th edn. London: Black.

Charlton, W. 1988. *Philosophy and Christian Belief*. London: Sheed and Ward.

Clark, B. 1978. *Whose Life Is It Anyway?*. London: Amber Lane Press.

Cohen, T. 1979. 'Metaphor and the Cultivation of Intimacy', in S. Sacks (ed.), *On Metaphor*. Chicago: University of Chicago Press.

Collins, A. 1737. *A Discourse of the Grounds and Reasons of the Christian Religion*. London.

Cooper, D. E. 1991. 'Ineffability', *Proceedings of the Aristotelian Society: Supplementary Volume* lxv, 1–15.

Copleston, F. 1946–1966. *A History of Philosophy*, 8 vols. London: Burns Oates.

Crichton, J. D. 1980. 'A Theology of Worship', in C. Jones, G. Wainwright and E. Yarnold (eds), *The Study of Liturgy*. London: SPCK.

Cupitt, D. 1990. *Creation out of Nothing*. London: SCM.

Davidson, D. 1967. 'Truth and Meaning', *Synthese* xvii, 304–23. Reprinted in Davidson 1984.

References

Davidson, D. 1974. 'On the Very Idea of a Conceptual Scheme', *Proceedings and Addresses of the American Philosophical Association* 47, 5–20. Reprinted in Davidson 1984.

Davidson, D. 1978. 'What Metaphors Mean', *Critical Inquiry* 5, 31–47. Reprinted in Davidson 1984.

Davidson, D. 1984. *Inquiries into Truth and Interpretation*. Oxford: Clarendon Press.

De Wulf, M. 1930. *Histoire de la philosophie médiévale*, Tome 3: *Après le tresième siècle*. Louvain: Institut de philosophie.

Dummett, M. 1978. *Truth and Other Enigmas*. London: Duckworth.

Dummett, M. 1991. *The Logical Basis of Metaphysics*. London: Duckworth.

Durrant, M. 1973a. *Theology and Intelligibility*. London: Routledge.

Durrant, M. 1973b. *The Logical Status of 'God'*. London: Macmillan.

Durrant, M. 1989. 'Reference and Critical Realism', *Modern Theology* 5, 2, 133–143.

Eckhart, J. 1936. *Meister Eckhart. Die deutchen Werke: erster band, Meister Eckhart's Predigten*. Stuttgart-Berlin: W. Kohlhammer.

Farrer, A. 1976. *Interpretation and Belief*, ed. C. C. Conti. London: SPCK.

Feuerbach, L. 1957. *The Essence of Christianity*, trans. G. Eliot. New York: Harper Torchbooks.

Frege, G. 1950. *The Foundations of Arithmetic*, trans. J. L. Austin. Oxford: Blackwell.

Frege, G. 1952. 'On Concept and Object', in *Translations from the Philosophical Writings of Gottlob Frege*, eds P. T. Geach and M. Black. Oxford: Blackwell.

Frei, H. W. 1974. *The Eclipse of Biblical Narrative: A Study in Eighteenth and Nineteenth Century Hermeneutics*. New Haven and London: Yale University Press.

Frost, D. L. 1973. *The Language of Series 3*. Bramcote: Grove Books.

Gadamer, H.-G. 1975. *Truth and Method*, trans. W. Glen-Doepel. London: Sheed and Ward.

Geach, P. T. 1962. *Reference and Generality: An Examination of Some Medieval and Modern Theories*. Ithaca, New York: Cornell University Press.

Geach, P. T. 1969. *God and the Soul*. London: Routledge.

Geach, P. T. 1979. *Truth, Love and Immortality: An Introduction to McTaggart's Philosophy*. London: Hutchinson.

Gibbs, B. 1976. 'Mysticism and the Soul', *The Monist* 59, 4, 532–50.

Gosse, E. 1935. *Father and Son: A Study of Two Temperaments*. London: Heinemann.

Greene, G. 1948. *The Heart of the Matter*. London: Heinemann.

Grice, H. P. 1968. 'Utterer's Meaning, Sentence-Meaning, and Word-Meaning', *Foundations of Language* 4, 225–242. Reprinted in Grice 1989.

Grice, H. P. 1975. 'Logic and Conversation', in P. Cole and J. L. Morgan (eds), *Syntax and Semantics*, vol. 3: Speech Acts. New York: Academic Press. Reprinted in Grice 1989.

Grice, H. P. 1989. *Studies in the Way of Words*. Cambridge, Mass. and London: Harvard University Press.

Griffiths, A. P. 1991. 'Kant's Psychological Hedonism', *Philosophy* 66, 207–216.

Hartshorne, C. 1969. 'The God of Religion and the God of Philosophy', in G. N. A. Vesey (ed.), *Talk of God*, Royal Institute of Philosophy Lectures. London and New York: Macmillan and St Martin's Press.

Holdcroft, D. 1981. 'Principles of Conversation, Speech Acts, and Radical Interpretation', in H. Parrett and J. Bouveresse (eds), *Meaning and Understanding*. Berlin and New York: Walter de Gruyter.

Holmyard, E. J. 1931. *Makers of Chemistry*. Oxford: Clarendon Press.

Houlden, J. L. 1974. 'Liturgy and her Companions: a Theological Appraisal', in R. C. D. Jasper (ed.), *The Eucharist Today: Studies on Series 3*. London: SPCK.

Ibsen, H. 1978. *Brand*, trans. G. Hill. London: Heinemann.

James, W. 1956. *The Will to Believe and other essays in popular philosophy*. New York: Dover.

Jenkins, D. E. 1967. *The Glory of Man*. London: SCM.

Jenkins, D. E. 1987. *God, Miracle and the Church of England*. London: SCM.

John of the Cross 1978. *The Complete Works of Saint John of the Cross*, trans. E. A. Pears. Wheathampstead: Clarke.

Kant, I. 1925. *Fundamental Principles of the Metaphysic of Ethics*, trans. T. K. Abbott. London: Longmans, Green and Co.

Kant, I. 1948. *The Moral Law or Kant's Groundwork of the Metaphysics of Morals*, trans. H. J. Paton. London: Hutchinson.

Karrer, O. (ed.) 1926 *Meister Eckehart*. Munich: J. Müller.

Kenny, A. 1967. 'Criterion', in P. Edwards (ed.), *The Encyclopedia of Philosophy*, 8 vols. New York and London: Macmillan.

Kenny, A. 1983. *Faith and Reason*. New York: Columbia University Press.

Kierkegaard, S. 1939. *Fear and Trembling*, trans. R. Payne. London: Oxford University Press.

Kierkegaard, S. 1954. *Fear and Trembling*, trans. W. Lowrie. New York: Doubleday Anchor Books.

Kirk, G. S., Raven, J. E. and Schofield, M. 1983. *The Presocratic Philosophers: A Critical History with a Selection of Texts*, 2nd edn. Cambridge: Cambridge University Press.

Kittay, E. F. 1987. *Metaphor: Its Cognitive Force and Linguistic Structure*. Oxford: Clarendon Press.

Kugel, J. L. 1981. *The Idea of Biblical Poetry: Parallelism and its History*. New Haven and London: Yale University Press.

Lamarque, P. 1982. 'Metaphor and Reported Speech: In Defence of a Pragmatic Theory', *Journal of Literary Semantics* 11, 14–18.

Lamarque, P. (ed.) 1983. *Philosophy and Fiction: Essays in Literary Aesthetics*. Aberdeen: Aberdeen University Press.

Lamarque, P. 1985. 'Philosophical Theories of Metaphor', *Studies in Philosophy* 10, 1–13.

Locke, J. 1959. *An Essay Concerning Human Understanding*, 2 vols, ed. A.C. Fraser. New York: Dover.

Malcolm, N. 1960. 'Anselm's Ontological Arguments', *The Philosophical Review*, 69, 41–62.

References

McCabe, H. 1987. *God Matters*. London: Chapman.

Millar, A. and Riches, J.K. 1981. 'Interpretation: A Theoretical Perspective and Some Applications', *Numen* xxviii, 1, 29–53.

Mitchell, B. 1973. *The Justification of Religious Belief*. London: Macmillan.

Mitchell, B. 1980. *Morality: Religious and Secular*. Oxford: Clarendon Press.

Mitchell, B. 1990. 'The Place of Symbols in Christianity', in his *How to Play Theological Ping-Pong and Other Essays on Faith and Reason*. London: Hodder & Stoughton.

Morris, T. V. (ed.) 1987a. *The Concept of God*. Oxford: Oxford University Press.

Morris, T. V. 1987b. 'The God of Abraham, Isaac and Anselm', in his *Anselmian Explorations: Essays in Philosophical Theology*. Indiana: University of Notre Dame Press.

Mortimer, J. 1991. 'The Monsignor at Ninety', *The Spectator* 6th July, 19–21.

Nicholas of Cusa 1913. *De docta ignorantia libri tres. Testo latino con note di Paolo Rotta*. Bari: G. Laterza.

Nietzsche, F. W. 1974. *The Gay Science*, trans. W. Kaufmann. New York: Vintage Books.

OED 1971. *The Compact Edition of the Oxford English Dictionary*, 2 vols. Oxford: Oxford University Press.

O'Hara, J. 1931. Contribution to BBC symposium *Science and Religion*, broadcast 1930. London: G. Howe .

Olsen, S. H. 1978. *The Structure of Literary Understanding*. Cambridge: Cambridge University Press.

Olsen, S. H. 1987. *The End of Literary Theory*. Cambridge: Cambridge University Press.

Pascal, B. 1966. *Pensées*, trans. A. J. Krailsheimer. Harmondsworth: Penguin.

Plantinga, A. 1967. *God and Other Minds: A Study of the Rational Justification of Belief in God*. Ithaca and London: Cornell University Press.

Plato 1963. *The Collected Dialogues of Plato, Including the Letters*, eds E. Hamilton and H. Cairns. New York: Bollingen Foundation.

Quinton, A. M. 1985. *The Divergence of the Twain: Poet's Philosophy and Philosopher's Philosophy*. Coventry: University of Warwick.

Rahner, H. 1955. 'The Christian Mystery and the Pagan Mysteries', in J. Campbell (ed.), *Pagan and Christian Mysteries: Papers from the Eranos Yearbooks*. New York: Harper and Row.

Ricoeur, P. 1969. *The Symbolism of Evil*, trans. E. Buchanan. Boston: Beacon Press.

Ricoeur, P. 1970. *Freud and Philosophy: An Essay on Interpretation*, trans. D. Savage. New Haven and London: Yale University Press.

Rorty, R. 1980. *Philosophy and the Mirror of Nature*. Oxford: Blackwell.

Rorty, R. 1982. *Consequences of Pragmatism (Essays: 1972–1980)*. Brighton: Harvester.

Rorty, R. 1989. *Contingency, Irony and Solidarity*. Cambridge: Cambridge University Press.

Ross, J. F. 1961. 'Analogy as a Rule of Meaning for Religious Language', *International Philosophical Quarterly* 1, 468–502.

Ross, J. F. 1981. *Portraying Analogy*. Cambridge: Cambridge University Press.

Russell, B. 1921. *Mysticism and Logic and Other Essays*. London: Longmans, Green & Co.

Sartre, J.-P. 1948. *Existentialism and Humanism*, trans. P. Mairet. London: Methuen.

Searle, J. R. 1979. 'Metaphor', in his *Expression and Meaning: Studies in the Theory of Speech Acts*. Cambridge: Cambridge University Press.

Smalley, B. 1952. *The Study of the Bible in the Middle Ages*. Oxford: Blackwell.

Smart, N. 1972. *The Concept of Worship*. London: Macmillan.

Soskice, J. M. 1985. *Metaphor and Religious Language*. Oxford: Clarendon Press.

Sperber, D. and Wilson, D. 1986. *Relevance: Communication and Cognition*. Oxford: Blackwell.

Strange, R. 1990. 'The Flame of Love: Reflections on Newman's "Dream of Gerontius"', *Priests and People* 4, 11, 442–445.

Strawson, P. F. 1969. 'Meaning and Truth'. Inaugural lecture at the University of Oxford. Reprinted in Strawson 1971.

Strawson, P. F. 1971. *Logico-Linguistic Papers*. London: Methuen

Sutherland, S. 1977. *Atheism and the Rejection of God: Contemporary Philosophy and The Brothers Karamazov*. Oxford: Blackwell .

Sutherland, S. 1980. 'Saintliness and Sanity', *Scottish Journal of Religious Studies* I, 1, 45–61.

Sutherland, S. 1984a. *Faith and Ambiguity*. London: SCM.

Sutherland, S. 1984b. *God, Jesus and Belief: The Legacy of Theism*. Oxford: Blackwell.

Thomas Aquinas 1936. *De Unitate Intellectus*, ed. L. W. Keeler. Rome: Gregorian University. (1946. *The Unicity of the Intellect*, trans. R.E. Brennan. St Louis: Herder.)

Thomas Aquinas 1964–81. *Summa Theologiae*, trans. T. Gilby and others, 60 vols. London and New York: Blackfriars, Eyre & Spottiswoode, McGraw-Hill.

Travis, C. 1991. 'Annals of Analysis', *Mind* c, 2, 236–64.

Trigg, R. H. 1973. *Reason and Commitment*. Cambridge: Cambridge University Press.

Trigg, R. H. 1985. *Understanding Social Science*. Oxford: Blackwell.

Trigg, R. H. 1988a. 'The Metaphysical Self', *Religious Studies* 24, 3, 277–89.

Trigg, R. H. 1988b. *Ideas of Human Nature*. Oxford: Blackwell.

Trigg, R. H. 1989. *Reality at Risk: A Defence of Realism in Philosophy and the Sciences*, 2nd edn. New York and London: Harvester.

Wainwright, G. 1980. 'The Understanding of Liturgy in the Light of its History', in C. Jones, G. Wainwright and E. Yarnold (eds), *The Study of Liturgy*. London: SPCK.

Warner, M. M. 1973. 'Black's Metaphors', *The British Journal of Aesthetics* 13, 367–372.

References

Warner, M. M. 1985. 'Philosophy, Language and the Reform of Public Worship', in A. Phillips Griffiths (ed.), *Philosophy and Practice. Royal Institute of Philosophy Lectures*. Cambridge: Cambridge University Press.

Warner, M. M. 1989a. *Philosophical Finesse: Studies in the Art of Rational Persuasion*. Oxford: Clarendon Press.

Warner, M. M. 1989b. 'On Not Deconstructing the Difference between Literature and Philosophy', *Philosophy and Literature* 13, 1, 16–27.

Warner, M. M. 1990a. 'Philosophy, Implicature and Liturgy', in D. Jasper & R. C. D. Jasper (eds), *Language and the Worship of the Church*. London: Macmillan.

Warner, M. M. (ed.) 1990b. *The Bible as Rhetoric: Studies in Biblical Persuasion and Credibility*. London and New York: Routledge.

Wittgenstein, L. 1933. *Tractatus Logico-Philosophicus*, trans. C. K. Ogden. London: Routledge & Kegan Paul.

Wittgenstein, L. 1953. *Philosophical Investigations*, trans. G. E. M. Anscombe. Oxford: Blackwell.

Wittgenstein, L. 1958. *The Blue and Brown Books*, ed. R. Rhees. Oxford: Blackwell.

Wittgenstein, L. 1961a. *Notebooks: 1914–1916*, ed. G. H. von Wright and G. E. M. Anscombe, trans. G. E. M. Anscombe. Oxford: Blackwell.

Wittgenstein, L. 1961b. *Tractatus Logico-Philosophicus*, trans. D. F. Pears and B. F. McGuinness. London: Routledge & Kegan Paul.

Wittgenstein, L. 1965. 'Wittgenstein's Lecture on Ethics', *The Philosophical Review*, lxxiv, 1, 3–26.

Wittgenstein, L. 1966. *Lectures and Conversations on Aesthetics, Psychology and Religious Belief*, ed. D. C. Barrett. Oxford: Blackwell.

Wittgenstein, L. 1967. *Wittgenstein und der Weiner Kreis*, recorded by F. Waismann, ed. B. F. McGuiness. Oxford: Blackwell.

Wittgenstein, L. 1969. *On Certainty*, ed. G. E. M. Anscombe and G. H. von Wright, trans. D. Paul and G. E. M. Anscombe. Oxford: Blackwell.

Wittgenstein, L. 1975. *Philosophical Remarks*, ed. R. Rhees, trans. R. Hargreaves and R. White. Oxford: Blackwell.

Wittgenstein, L. 1979. *Wittgenstein and the Vienna Circle*, recorded by F. Waismann, ed. B. F. McGuiness, trans. J. Schulte and B. F. McGuiness. Oxford: Blackwell .

Wittgenstein, L. 1980. *Culture and Value*, ed. G. H. von Wright, trans. P. Winch. Oxford: Blackwell.

Wood, T. 1986. 'Euthanasia', in J. Macquarrie and J. Childress (eds), *A New Dictionary of Christian Ethics*. London: SCM Press.

Index

Abraham, 13, 19, 20 75–8, 124–6, 129–32, 138–42, 145n.
analogy, 1, 3, 11–12, 15, 16, 18, 21, 45, 57–9, 64–7, 96, 97–100, 102–3, 138
Anselm, St, 7, 13, 14, 19, 47, 64, 75–81, 87, 137
anti-realism, *see* realism
Aristotle, 31, 46, 50, 54, 64, 71n., 73, 99
Arnold, T., 123
atheism, *see* theism
Augustine, St, 15, 17, 63, 91–3, 96–8, 102, 104, 105, 107–8, 111, 113–15, 117, 119, 141
Austin, J. L., 100–1
authority, 16, 23, 25, 92–3, 95–7, 99, 104, 106, 108, 115–16, 120, 122
Ayer, A. J., 61, 69n.

Bambrough, J. R., 3, 6, 23–32, 33
Bambrough, M., 28n.
Barrett, D. C., 7–9, 11–15, 61–9
Barth, K., 63, 64, 67
belief, *see* faith
Bell, M., 100
Berkeley, G., 4, 38, 64
Bible, *see* Scripture
biblical references, 1, 2, 7, 9, 12, 20, 61, 75, 84n., 89–92, 94–9, 105, 107–8, 110–11, 133, 137, 139–41, 145–6
Bishop of Durham, *see* Jenkins, D. E.
Bochenski, I. M., 66
Brooks, C., 118–19
Burnet, J., 88

cause, 10, 12–13, 21, 35, 48–53, 58, 71n., 81–2, 99, 102, 123
Charlton, W., 83
choice, 1, 2, 5, 27–32, 35
Christ, *see* Jesus

Christianity, 1–2, 13–14, 16, 18, 20, 39, 41–2, 71–3, 75–80, 82, 87, 88, 90, 91, 92, 95, 96, 103, 104–7, 116, 121n., 122, 129, 130, 132, 141
Clark, B., 128–30
Cohen, T., 119
Collins, A., 94
Cooper, D. E., 103n.
Copleston, F., 61–2
creation, 1, 5, 6, 10–15, 21, 27, 35–7, 40, 51–3, 57, 59, 63, 75–9, 82, 86, 87, 99, 105, 129, 133, 137, 144
Crichton, J. D., 105
criterion, 2, 8, 21
Cupitt, D., 5–7, 37, 39–42

Davidson, D., 12, 95, 100
deism, 94–6, 106
Descartes, R., 56, 84n., 86–7
De Wulf, M., 62
dichotomies, 3, 5, 15, 20, 23, 26, 27, 33, 41, 53
divine, *see* God
Dummett, M., 4, 6
Durrant, M., 10n., 13–15, 71–84, 85–7

Eckhart, J., 11, 61–2, 69
Eliot, T. S., 21
Enlightenment, the, 2, 5, 15, 17, 37, 41, 94, 96, 98, 99, 107, 109–10, 117
Ernst, C., 54
esse, 9–11, 45, 51–5, 64
ethics, 2, 11, 18–21, 26, 29, 61, 63, 96, 123–46
evil, 2, 12, 26

faith, 1, 3, 5–7, 11, 13, 16–18, 20, 23–32, 33–5, 37–9, 41–3, 49, 58, 68, 75, 76, 80, 87, 93, 95, 96, 97, 100, 104–5, 107, 108, 114, 115, 116, 119, 123–7, 131–2, 136, 137, 139–40, 143–5

Index